The Critical Idiom

General Editor: JOHN D. JUMP

28 Melodrama

In the same series

Melodrama/*James L. Smith*

Methuen & Co Ltd

First published 1973
by Methuen & Co Ltd
11 New Fetter Lane London EC4
© *1973 James L. Smith*
Printed in Great Britain
by Cox & Wyman Ltd, Fakenham, Norfolk

· LC # 74 - 164331

ISBN 0 416 79330 4 Hardback
ISBN 0 416 79340 1 Paperback

Distributed in the U.S.A. by
HARPER & ROW PUBLISHERS, INC.
BARNES & NOBLE IMPORT DIVISION

For my mother

Contents

General Editor's Preface

The volumes composing the Critical Idiom deal with a wide variety of key terms in our critical vocabulary. The purpose of the series differs from that served by the standard glossaries of literary terms. Many terms are adequately defined for the needs of students by the brief entries in these glossaries, and such terms do not call for attention in the present series. But there are other terms which cannot be made familiar by means of compact definitions. Students need to grow accustomed to them through simple and straightforward but reasonably full discussions. The main purpose of this series is to provide such discussions.

Many critics have borrowed methods and criteria from currently influential bodies of knowledge or belief that have developed without particular reference to literature. In our own century, some of them have drawn on art-history, psychology, or sociology. Others, strong in a comprehensive faith, have looked at literature and literary criticism from a Marxist or a Christian or some other sharply defined point of view. The result has been the importation into literary criticism of terms from the vocabularies of these sciences and creeds. Discussions of such bodies of knowledge and belief in their bearing upon literature and literary criticism form a natural extension of the initial aim of the Critical Idiom.

Because of their diversity of subject-matter, the studies in the series vary considerably in structure. But all authors have tried to give as full illustrative quotation as possible, to make reference whenever appropriate to more than one literature, and to write in such a way as to guide readers towards the short bibliographies in which they have made suggestions for further reading.

John D. Jump

University of Manchester

I
The Nature of Melodrama

What is melodrama? In 1913 William Gillette confessed that even when he questioned 'really intellectual people' none of them 'appeared to be certain'. The situation has not changed. Ask a musician, or a literary scholar, or even that convenient abstraction the man in the street. You will get three very different answers.

The first melodrama, the musician points out, was *Pygmalion*, a brief *scène lyrique* with libretto by Jean Jacques Rousseau. The plot is simplicity itself: Pygmalion chips away at his statue of Galathée, the marble comes to life, breathes a few words (mostly 'moi') and sinks into the arms of her astonished creator as the curtain falls. The novelty lies in Rousseau's method of linking words with music. He thought French too harsh a language to be sung and for *Pygmalion* devised instead a kind of musical leap-frog:

> un genre de drame, dans lequel les paroles et la musique, au lieu de marcher ensemble, se font entendre successivement, et où la phrase parlée est en quelque sorte annoncée et préparée par la phrase musicale. [a type of drama in which words and music, instead of going together, are heard alternately, and where the spoken phrase is, as it were, announced and prepared by the musical phrase.]
>
> (*Observations sur l'Alceste de M. Gluck*, 1774, *Oeuvres complètes*, Paris, 1836–37, III. 563)

Thus while Pygmalion broods in silence, music expresses his dejection; when he speaks, it stops; he takes up the chisel, and it starts again. The idea caught on. *Pygmalion* was performed at Lyons in 1770, at Weimar in 1772 and took Paris by storm in

1775. Goethe praised it, and Georg Benda paid it the compliment of imitation in his *Ariadne auf Naxos* (1774). So did Florian, whose *Héro et Léandre* (1785) shows the heroine anxiously monologuing at Sestos while a storm lashes the Hellespont and Léandre is glimpsed sinking beneath the waves. Meanwhile, Benda carried the experiment further in his *Medea* (1775), with dialogue spoken not in between but over the music. It became necessary to distinguish such works from opera proper, and the term to hand was *mélodrame*. The word derives from the Greek *melos* (music), and with this root meaning of music-drama was a common eighteenth-century synonym for opera – a meaning which the Italian *melodramma* retains today. Rousseau still thought of *mélodrame* as opera in 1774, for he declared in the *Observations* that *Pygmalion* had created a new genre mid-way between simple declamation and 'le véritable mélodrame'. But by 1785 Florian was writing of his *Héro* as a 'mélodrame', and Benda's *Ariadne* was so entitled when it appeared in Paris in 1781. By the turn of the century the semantic shift was complete, and *melodrama* meant what for the musician it means today: 'a play, or a passage in a play, or a poem, in which the spoken voice is used against a musical background' (Percy A. Scholes, *The Oxford Companion to Music*, 9th edition, 1955, p. 624). Curiously enough, Rousseau's invention and Benda's extension of it can still be heard today. Mozart's opera *Zaïde* has two melodramas embedded in it, and Beethoven uses one in the grave-digging scene of *Fidelio* and another at the end of *Egmont*. Weber, Schumann and Bizet have all written melodramas; so has Poulenc whose *La Voix humaine* presents a modern Ariadne desperately calling up her lover on the telephone.

Meanwhile, Rousseau's *mélodrame* had been swallowed whole by that voracious python the Boulevard du Temple, where since 1670 fit-up booths had entertained the Parisian mob with tumblers, jugglers, stiltwalkers, rope-dancers, puppeteers, magicians, infant prodigies, freaks and animals, harlequinades, fairy-tales adapted from Perrault and spectacular musical pantomimes on mythical, historic or contemporary themes, performed in dumbshow with explanatory placards to aid the understanding. Fragments of dialogue, transforming pantomime into *pantomime dialoguée*, crept into Ribié's *La Prise de Mitylène*, performed under Arnould-Mussot at his magnificent Théâtre de l'Ambigu-Comique. Here in 1785 was staged Florian's *Galathée*, a bastard *mélodrame* with dialogue in rhymed couplets, elaborate pantomime, a '*ballet général*' and musical numbers set to popular operatic airs cribbed from Sedaine's music-drama *Richard Coeur-de-Lion*. 1792 brought a version of Schiller's *Die Räuber*, and 1800 *Cœlina ou l'Enfant du mystère*, with which Guilbert de Pixerécourt established overnight the pattern of popular melodrama for the next hundred years.

Almost everything in *Cœlina* was borrowed, and not only from the romance of the same title by Ducray-Duminil which provided Pixerécourt with his first two acts. The rugged mountain scenery of Act Three, complete with distant peaks, foaming river, 'practical' bridge and rustic millhouse, was first built for Schiller. Boulevard pantomime provides the action-packed but almost wordless finale, and a mute old man who 'talks' by means of dumbshow. The singing miller and clodhopping peasantry appear by courtesy of Sedaine's music-drama, which also siphons off the 'comic relief' into separate characters remote from the main action. But the greatest debt is to the *drame*, that genre of serious prose tragicomedy which derives its sentimentality from Cumberland and its bourgeois didacticism from the horrible homilies of George Lillo. For excitement and suspense, *Cœlina* relies heavily on such well-worn devices as long-lost children, lying letters, tell-tale scars, secret marriages, murders frustrated and plots overheard – all of them readily available in Cumberland's comedies, where Pixerécourt could also have discovered his *dramatis personae*. Augusta Aubrey, Cumberland's much-harassed heroine in *The Fashionable Lover* is, like Cœlina, a wretched orphan driven from the sheltering roof, robbed of her fortune by a villainous uncle and pestered by unwanted attentions ('resistance is in vain; if you refuse my favours, Madam, you shall feel my force'). Both plays have a handsome and courageous hero, a comic servant who befriends innocence in distress and a mysterious stranger, later revealed as the heroine's long-lost father ('Gracious Providence, this is too much!'). Such providential platitudes, and a liberal garnish of moral maxims, are another common element, but the two dramatists differ on questions of practical justice. Cumberland's rake Lord Abberville, like many a villain of the *drame*, is allowed to escape punishment by a timely reformation at the final curtain ('I have been lost in error'). Pixerécourt has no truck with such sentimental palliatives. His Truguelin is arrested and sent for trial, after suffering agonies of conscience in the electric atmosphere of an Alpine thunderstorm:

> *Il parcourt le théâtre comme un insensé.* Où fuir? où porter ma honte et mes remords? . . . Il me semble que tout, dans la nature, se réunit pour m'accuser. Ces mots terribles retentissent sans cesse à mon oreille: point de repos pour l'assassin! vengeance! vengeance! [*He wanders about the stage like a madman.* Whither shall I fly? where shall I take my shame and my remorse? . . . I feel as though everything in nature conspires to accuse me. Those terrible words resound unceasingly in my ear: no rest for the murderer! vengeance! vengeance!]

Pixerécourt blended his ingredients shrewdly. *Cœlina* was a great theatrical success. It ran for 387 performances on the Boulevard, was translated into Dutch, German and English, and in 1802 appeared at Covent Garden as *A Tale of Mystery*. This adaptation, by Thomas Holcroft, calls for extensive background music to heighten entrances, indicate character and underline the mood of a scene. The first act alone asks for '*soft music*', '*sweet and cheerful music*', '*confused music*', '*threatening music*', '*music to express discontent and alarm*', '*music of doubt and terror*' and much more besides. Pixerécourt published *Cœlina* in 1800 as a 'drame en trois actes, en prose, et à grand spectacle' ['spectacular prose drama in three acts'].

Holcroft published *A Tale of Mystery* in 1802 as a 'melo-drame'. Thousands of melodramas appeared on the English stage during the nineteenth century; gradually their musical element dwindled into insignificance, and eventually it disappeared altogether. But the name remained, and *melodrama* thus came to mean what the Oxford English Dictionary understands by the term: 'a dramatic piece characterized by sensational incident and violent appeals to the emotions, but with a happy ending'. This cool definition has been conveniently expanded by Frank Rahill in *The World of Melodrama* (Pennsylvania, 1967):

> Melodrama is a form of dramatic composition in prose partaking of the nature of tragedy, comedy, pantomime, and spectacle, and intended for a popular audience. Primarily concerned with situation and plot, it calls upon mimed action extensively and employs a more or less fixed complement of stock characters, the most important of which are a suffering heroine or hero, a persecuting villain, and a benevolent comic. It is conventionally moral and humanitarian in point of view and sentimental and optimistic in temper, concluding its fable happily with virtue rewarded after many trials and vice punished. Characteristically it offers elaborate scenic accessories and miscellaneous divertissements and introduces music freely, typically to underscore dramatic effect. (p. xiv)

Behind this formulation, which might be a point-for-point summary of *A Tale of Mystery*, lie all the tawdry splendours of the Victorian melodrama. Here they are, touting for custom in the staccato phrases of some contemporary playbills:

THRILLING INCIDENTS! STARTLING SITUATIONS. ROBBERY
AT THE MANSION! THE RAILWAY MURDER. THE PERILS OF
THE STEAM SAW MILL. False Denunciation! Arrest of the inno-
cent! TERRIFIC LONG SWORD COMBAT! Julian Overpowered by
the Pirates. NOVELTY UNPRECEDENTED! Terrific and Powerful
Effects. LAKE OF TRANSPARENT ROLLING FIRE! THE SKELETON
MONK! AFFLICTION AND REMORSE! The Suffering Wife, The
dissipated Husband, and the Sick Child. Luke and the Seducer!
TERRIBLE DEGRADATION OF AGNES! LADY HATTON LEADS A
LIFE OF PIETY. '*ARCHIBALD, will you not bless me before I
die?*' '*Give me back my Husband.*' WONDERFUL DENOUEMENT!
The Rescue of Emma Deane. THE DEFENCE OF THE CONSULATE.
'*You may take my life—But you cannot take from me my Victoria
Cross.*' *TRIUMPH OF THE BRITISH FLAG OVER
SLAVERY.* The Real Murderer Discovered. CORNERED! THE
LIBERTINE DESTROYED. DEATH BY POISON. JUDGMENT OVER-
TAKES THE GUILTY! The execution. The Death Struggle! DES-
TRUCTION OF THE MURDERER BY THE FANGS OF THE FAITHFUL
DOG. *HOME SWEET HOME.*

The plays so described range from *My Poll and My Partner Joe*
(1835) to *The Great World of London* (1898). Under their influence *melodrama* has joined the long list of once-precise words
hopelessly debased by popular misuse. No longer does it suggest
the dramatic genre invented by Pixerécourt. It is a term which
the man in the street loosely applies to any machine-made enter-
tainment dealing in vulgar extravagance, implausible motivation,
meretricious sensation and spurious pathos. Even William Archer
used it in this sense in *The Old Drama and the New* (1923), when
he exalted the modern drama of Archer, Pinero and Shaw by
debasing what he called 'the general ruck of Elizabethan melodramas' (p. 100). These apparently include *The Revenger's
Tragedy* – a 'monstrous melodrama' (p. 74) – and *The Duchess
of Malfi* – a sequence of 'crude and arbitrary horrors which would
be hooted or laughed off the stage if a melodramatist of today
dared to offer them to his public' (p. 61). In short, *melodrama*

has in popular use become a blanket term of abuse and contempt. It is probably the dirtiest word a drama critic dare print.

Surprisingly, modern scholars not attempting denigration have often echoed Archer's descriptions, and even applied them more widely. Handbooks of dramatic terms list as melodramas works by such tragic dramatists as Aeschylus and Euripides, Shakespeare, Tourneur and Webster, Otway, Lillo, Schiller, Gorky, Ibsen, Synge, O'Neill and Arthur Miller. What possible meaning can be attached to *melodrama* in such a context? Can any real similarities exist between plays as diverse as *The Persians*, *Medea*, *Richard III*, *The Revenger's Tragedy*, *The Duchess of Malfi*, *The Orphan*, *The London Merchant*, *Die Räuber*, *The Lower Depths*, *An Enemy of the People*, *Riders to the Sea*, *The Iceman Cometh* and *Death of a Salesman*? And what can such plays have in common with *East Lynne* and *Lady Audley's Secret*, *Black-ey'd Susan* and *The Bells*? I believe it is possible to show that these exciting Victorian dramas share with many Greek, Elizabethan and modern 'tragedies' a fundamentally melodramatic view of life, which conditions their organic form and dictates the emotional responses of an audience.

In *Tragedy and Melodrama* (Seattle, 1968), Robert Bechtold Heilman argues persuasively that tragic man is essentially 'divided' and melodramatic man essentially 'whole'. Antigone cannot bury her brother without offending civil law, Orestes and Hamlet cannot avenge their fathers' deaths without committing murder, Macbeth cannot gain the crown without violating moral sanctions which he respects. In tragedy therefore, 'no villain need be'; in Meredith's fine phrase man is 'betrayed by what is false within'. In melodrama man remains undivided, free from the agony of choosing between conflicting imperatives and desires. He greets every situation with an unwavering single impulse which absorbs his whole personality. If there is danger he is courageous, if there is political corruption he exposes it, untroubled by cowardice, weakness or doubt, self-interest or thought of self-preservation. By itself, such 'wholeness' is morally uncommitted: Shelley's Count Cenci is as totally devoted to evil as Ibsen's Dr Stockmann is to good. Both are debarred from that growth in personal awareness brought about by the *anagnorisis* or discovery of tragedy: the evil man who is wholly evil is prevented by his wholeness from the self-understanding that might curb his villainy, and the wholly good man who looks inward has nothing to contemplate but his own virtuous perfection. It follows that the undivided protagonist of melodrama has only external pressures to fight against: an evil man, a social group, a hostile ideology, a natural force, an accident or chance, an obdurate fate or a malign deity. It is this total dependence upon external adversaries which finally separates melodrama from all other serious dramatic forms. *Oedipus Rex* and *The Persians* both deal in human suffering, but Oedipus' agonies are brought about by his own *hubris* while the Persians are helpless victims of a vast military disaster. Sophocles wrote tragedy and Aeschylus melodrama. Or, from the seventeenth century, compare *Phèdre* and *The Duchess of Malfi*. Racine's heroine is destroyed by her own divided passions; Webster's duchess – despite her social and perhaps moral peccadilloes – by the machinations of her evil brothers. Racine wrote tragedy and Webster melodrama. One play deals with self-knowledge, the other with self-preservation; one is concerned with restructuring relations with the universe, the other with restructuring relations with other people or events or things.

Characteristically, melodrama presses its own extreme conflicts to extreme conclusions. Only three are possible, for when an undivided protagonist opposes a hostile world – whether in real life or on the stage – the result must be stalemate, victory or defeat. Thus in the real-life conflict of man against nature, Crowhurst withdraws from the struggle between his one-man catamaran and the cruel sea, Hillary plants a Union Jack on the summit of Everest, and Captain Scott perishes in the blizzards of Antarctica. So in the theatre, where the eternal stalemate of Sartre's *Huis clos* is rare, an avalanche crushes Ibsen's Brand but not the indestructible heroine of Boucicault's *Pauvrette*, strong tides rob Maurya of all her sons in Synge's *Riders to the Sea* but the fight to save a life threatened by natural accidents is always successful in *The Doctors*, evil men strangle Webster's duchess but Cœlina lives to see Trugeulin arrested, far-fetched coincidence brings about the unlucky deaths of Romeo and Juliet but saves from execution at the yardarm William the sailor hero of *Black-ey'd Susan*. The essential point is that resolutions of triumph or defeat indicate not different dramatic structures but simply alternative formulations of the same conflict, opposite extremes of the same melodramatic spectrum.

Such clear-cut endings offer an audience emotional pleasures equally clear-cut and extreme. Sailor William gains everything: life, liberty and the pursuit of happiness with his beloved Susan. We rejoice at his luck, share vicariously in his triumphs and leave the theatre ready to tackle the world single-handed and win. The Persians, by contrast, lose everything and we pity their loss. Aeschylus' play deals exclusively in overwhelming disaster; everything invites us to give up and go under, to abandon hope, embrace despair, and surrender to the luxurious solace of a really good cry. Dr Stockmann loses too, but because he goes down fighting, our pity is swallowed up in righteous anger at the inflexible selfishness of his destroyers. This time we leave the theatre militant crusaders against municipal corruption and graft. Triumph, despair and protest are the basic emotions of melo-drama, and the art of working each to its highest pitch occasions the *catharsis* of the form. The chapters which follow examine the dramatic structures of each emotion in turn; my point here is that in melodrama these emotions are savoured singly and in isolation, divorced from anything which might qualify, contradict or otherwise diminish what Heilman calls the prevailing 'monopathic' tone. We enjoy triumph without considering its cost to others, despair without seeking for alternative courses, and protest without questioning the bases of our own superior moral integrity. Here is the final contrast with tragedy, where resolutions are always complex. In melodrama we win or lose; in tragedy we lose in the winning like Oedipus Rex or Macbeth, or win in the losing like Hamlet or Antony and Cleopatra.

A dramatic form which pits an undivided protagonist against external adversity, and resolves the conflict with an extreme solution designed to produce an overwhelmingly monopathic *catharsis*, may seem naïve, trivial and second-rate, especially when compared with the rich complexities and broader moral dimensions of tragedy. But to dismiss melodrama on these grounds is dangerously oversimple. The fact that most of the serious plays ever written have been melodramas and not tragedies points to a second and more important fact: that we see most of the serious conflicts and crises of our everyday lives in melodramatic, rather than tragic, terms. The destructive agonies of tragic dividedness are not for every day and the seductive pleasures of melodramatic wholeness are everywhere available. It is comforting to lay the blame for our failure on other shoulders, and shrink from the rigours of self-castigation into the euphoric illusion that we are innocent victims of a hostile world. Again, it is heartening to cast private doubt and reservation aside, and enter wholeheartedly into a struggle against manifest injustice. By attacking villains we can all become heroes. Corporate campaigning is even more wholesome, for when others share our beliefs we must be right. Whether we support 'Spurs or Arsenal, Cowboys or Indians, Labour or Conservative, Democrat or Republican, North or South, Protestant or Catholic, East or West, is here immaterial: the important fact is that we take a side and accept its credo.

Painful decisions can be left to the leaders who formulate policy. We function as loyal supporters who rally round the flag and repel the opposition. These exhilarating tussles are often fought to a truly melodramatic finish: a football match, like an election campaign, a battle or a war, must be lost or won. If there is deadlock, we demand a replay. And afterwards there is the pleasurable monopathy of triumph or defeat, or even the aggressive comfort of blaming the referee. In short, melodrama is the dramatic form which expresses the reality of the human condition as we all experience it most of the time.

The aesthetic expression of this view of life need not be trivial and second-rate. To be sure, melodrama is responsible for a great deal of popular trash, but this does not mean that *all* melodrama must be trashy. Like any genre, it affords a wide range of excellence.

Look, for example, at the melodrama of war. Triumph here will embrace the flight of refugee children across tricky terrain; the escape of daring prisoners from barbed-wire compounds, Alsatian wolf-hounds and sadistic guards; or the dogged resistance of decimated troops surrounded and outnumbered by the confident foe. The result may be as sentimental as *The Sound of Music*, as adventurous as *The Great Escape* or as trite as *Tommy Atkins*, where a cliché-ridden curate called Harold Wilson rallies the defenders of a besieged garrison in the Sudan with:

> Comrades, will you follow me? *(He is answered by a ringing cheer.)* We are only a handful against an enemy numbering their Thousands – There is *no* hope of *Victory*, I will lead you to *Death*!! If we surrender they might spare our lives. We might return home to those who are near and dear to us – but at the price of dishonour. . . . You do not flinch? *(General dissent.)* Then follow me. And we'll show the enemy How British bulldogs die! Sound the advance!!

In *Jessie Brown*, on the other hand, Boucicault lifts this stock situation into something approaching art. It is the siege of

Lucknow. The enemy are still mere 'scum', the English officers still gallant gentlemen, and the other ranks still regional comedians radiating chipper confidence. But this is no musical-comedy war. The English ladies tearing up dresses for bandages look 'pale and worn', the men haggard and unshaven. One junior officer is secretly petrified with fear, and even bonnie Jessie, that 'sprig of heather from the Highland moors', find her public cheerfulness undermined by tears and uncontrollable hysteria. Such humanizing detail makes us care. The plight of the besieged outpost becomes more plausible, its defence more heroic and its relief more melo-dramatically triumphant.

Shakespeare uses the same trick. It is fashionable to see Henry V either as a man deeply divided against himself, or as a chilly, over-perfect king propelled by the Church into an indefensible foreign campaign for which he refuses to accept full moral responsibility. These unheroic views of the play fall down heavily before Agincourt, where the need for a united stand against fearful odds binds into a fatalistic freemasonry nobles and commons, Irish firebrands, Welsh pedants and canny Scotsmen, all under a royal captain who commends his private misgivings to God and heartens his men without minimizing their danger. The staggering victory of this ruined band, as intellectually implausible as it is emotionally convincing, creates a monopathy of triumph so overwhelming it can bring an audience close to tears.

Protest has its great moments too. Consider the savage indigna-tion of Charles Chilton's *Oh What a Lovely War*. A company of seaside pierrots sing jolly little songs about Fred Karno's Army while on a giant screen behind them we see banner headlines ('AVERAGE LIFE OF A MACHINE GUNNER UNDER ATTACK – FOUR MINUTES') and sickening newsreel photographs of the gassed, the bloody, the wounded, the limbless and the dead, a German soldier staring sightlessly up at the sky, or a green hillside covered with nothing but white wooden crosses as far as the eye can see. Or weigh the incendiary effect of Piscator's cool epilogue to his dramatization of *War and Peace*: 'In 1870 and 1871 a million people died. In 1914 to 1918 fifteen million. 1939 to 1945 fifty-five million. How much longer?' Or the speech of Ulysses to Hector which lies at the heart of Giraudoux's *La Guerre de Troie n'aura pas lieu*, retitled in the Christopher Fyr translation used here, *Tiger at the Gates*:

> It's usual on the eve of every war, for the two leaders of the peoples concerned to meet privately at some innocent village, on a terrace in a garden overlooking a lake. And they decide together that war is the world's worst scourge, and as they watch the rippling reflexions in the water, with magnolia petals dropping on to their shoulders, they are both of them peace-loving, modest and friendly. . . . And the next day war breaks out.

But the play which most savagely exposes the stupid suffering and futile carnage of war is Brecht's masterpiece, *Mother Courage*. In the wings, Protestant and Catholic fight out their Thirty Year Stalemate. On the stage, their reversals and victories are viewed only as threats to the survival of the cooks and camp-followers who cluster round Mother Courage's provision wagon. She sees clearly enough that black-market capitalists are the only real victors, that heroism springs from stupidity, brutality and error, and that only by bribery, guile and undeviating cowardice can she keep her bastard family alive and fed. Paradoxically, she is herself a petty profiteer living off the war, and while she haggles for better terms her children lapse into acts of bravery, honesty and compassion which always prove fatal. The play ends with Courage alone once more, harnessed between the shafts of her lightened wagon. Animated only by the will to survive, she has learned nothing and forgotten nothing, a cunning stupid victim of an endlessly futile campaign.

The figure ranks powerfully beside those more innocent victims of defeat, *The Trojan Women*. Troy lies in ruins, its army slain, its elders butchered, its womenfolk sacrificed like Polyxena to the dead or awaiting deportation as slaves and concubines of the all-conquering Greeks. Cassandra may prophesy Odysseus' stormy wanderings and the death awaiting Agamemnon, but there is no hope that Troy will rise again. The god Poseidon has abandoned his beloved altars, and Hector's son Astyanax is torn from his mother's arms and dashed to pieces lest the city find another hero. As trumpets recall the Greek soldiers to their ships and the towers of Ilium crash in flames, Hecuba and the chorus of Trojan women see plainly for the first time the totality of the collective doom which awaits them. By presenting the Greek spokesman as a sensitive and reluctant assassin, and by allowing Hecuba a flare of murderous hatred against Helen, the only begetter of this holocaust, Euripides invests his play with a psychological truthfulness which takes it beyond Aeschylus' purely formalized rhetoric of despair in *The Persians*. *The Trojan Women* must rank as the greatest melodrama of military disaster ever written.

My conclusion is plain. Any art form deserves to be judged by its highest, not by its lowest achievements. We value epic not for Horne's *Orion* but for Homer's *Odyssey*. We value tragedy not for Johnson's *Irene* but for *Oedipus Rex* and *King Lear*. We should value melodrama not for *Tommy Atkins* and *The Great Escape*, but for *Henry V*, *Mother Courage* and *The Trojan Women*. These plays represent the peaks of melodramatic triumph, protest and defeat. It is time now to consider more closely the undulating foothills of the form.

2
Triumph

There is a simple formula for making a play which will give its audience the easy pleasures of vicarious triumph. Take an innocent man and a defenceless woman, both of them wholly admirable and free from fault. Present them sympathetically, so that an audience will identify with them and share their hopes. And then set against them every obstacle you can devise. Persecute them with villains, dog them with ill-luck, thrust them into a hostile world which threatens at every moment their instant annihilation. Dramatize these excitements as effectively as the resources of the stage will allow, heighten the suspense with music, relieve it with laughter and tears. And then, when all seems lost, allow your hero and heroine to win. Let villainy be outwitted, ill-luck reversed, physical danger overcome and virtue finally rewarded with infinite joy. Present your play honestly, without condescension, and its warm and simple message will help every spectator to face life more courageously than before. This is the pattern of the melodrama of triumph. It can be found in every age, but is in none so well defined as the nineteenth century, when history brought together an audience eager for such plays and a theatre whose economic and technical resources were uniquely qualified to provide them.

The Industrial Revolution swept up into the cities of Europe a vast workforce of uneducated country people who sweated over noisy machines for starvation wages, slept six or eight to a room in slum dwelling-houses, and were back on the factory floor by five the next morning. Pulp literature offered no escape, for they could not read. And the cinema, like radio and television, had not yet been invented. Only the Church, the brothel, the circus, the public-house and the theatre remained, and of these the theatre was perhaps the most widely available and by far the most entertaining. To the theatre then they came, an invading army of factory slaves, navvies, guttersnipes, emaciated counter-clerks and care-worn women suckling babes in arms. And the theatre took them in. Covent Garden was rebuilt in 1792 to house an audience of over 3,000; Drury Lane in 1794 held 2,500; the Royal Coburg (1816) 2,800 and the Whitechapel Pavilion (1828) over 3,500. Between 1850 and 1860 the number of theatres in the country doubled, and by the mid-sixties London alone could seat over 150,000 people on a single night. As the politer sections of the audience withdrew in disorder to the seclusion of the bourgeois drawing-room and the educated delights of Mudie's circulating library, the mob that dominated the auditorium dictated what should be shown on the stage.

At Covent Garden and Drury Lane performing monkeys playing banjoes were more popular than Kemble and Kean playing the classics. When Macready made his Covent Garden début in 1816 *Othello* shared the bill with *Aladdin*, and in 1881 what Drury Lane lost on the Saxe-Meiningen *Julius Caesar* it recouped the next Christmas with *Sinbad the Sailor*. With the Haymarket for summer seasons, these two 'patent' houses preserved until 1843 the legal monopoly on all legitimate drama in the City of London. At the new 'minor' theatres even the classical repertoire could appear only in burletta-form, truncated to three acts with at least five musical items in each. Worse still, the new stages were so vast, and the gallery so remote, that every effect had to be exaggerated: fine comic pointing and intimate speech degenerated into broad gesture and rant. Thus emasculated and vulgarized, Shakespeare and Sheridan fell before eye-glutting spectacle and screaming farce. *Macbeth* and *The School for Scandal* were no rivals for *Abd el Kador, the Napoleon of Algeria* and *Did You Ever Send Your Wife to Camberwell?* Added to the limitations of a rowdy audience, a crippling legal system and a cavernous auditorium were the restricting pruderies of Victorian censorship, which found it necessary to delete from *Othello* the phrase 'O God! O heavenly God!' and denied ardent lovers the modest pleasure of calling their mistresses 'angels'. Inevitably, serious writers turned their backs upon the stage and theatre managers were constrained to hire commercial hacks who could cobble up a hasty piece to meet the scenery in stock, the talents of the resident company and the current craze of the town.

The mob that paid the piper called the tune. And they wanted more than custard pies and spangles, farce and pantomime. They wanted to forget the drudgery and drabness of everyday life and escape into a more colourful, less complex and plainly perfect world: where startling and marvellous adventures could arouse the most elemental feelings and loyalties without making any tiresome demands upon the mind; where situations could be summed up at a glance, characters represented obvious good or evil, and conflicts were always clear-cut; where chance and coincidence were brought under control, unlucky accidents overcome, and virtue after many thrilling reversals always triumphed over vice and received eminently satisfactory material rewards. In fact, they wanted the melodrama of triumph. And since in the theatre supply is always equal to demand, that is exactly what they got: 'a dream world' in Michael Booth's terms 'inhabited by dream people and dream justice, offering audiences the fulfilment and satisfaction found only in dreams' (*English Melodrama* (1965), p. 14). Once this underlying pattern is grasped, the apparently chaotic and absurd elements of popular melodrama – its stock characters, absurd plot, episodic structure, perfunctory style, scenic marvels, musical background, comic relief and rigid poetic justice – all fall inevitably into place. This chapter examines each in turn, and then discusses some variations and developments which add colour to the picture.

Dream people come first, for without people there is no play. You always know where you are with the characters of Victorian melodrama. A complete set of two-dimensional stereotypes, all sharply defined and all different, they are the 'whole' men who can be guaranteed to think, speak and act exactly as you would expect. No time is lost footling about with motivation, for there is no pretence that these are real people. A single epithet defines them. 'The wretch Malvoglio has deposed that good Francisco is the brother of the vile Romaldi' declares *A Tale of Mystery*. The very blankness of 'good Francisco' is an asset. You have to work hard to identify with the complex personal idiosyncrasies of Hedda Gabler or King Lear, but good Francisco does what anyone would do in his situation, and thus affords an audience the pleasure of instant and complete identification. Type-cast from the cradle, his fellows are even christened in character. A sycophant? Crawley. A drinking companion? Hockaday. A bailiff? Sam Snatchem. A carpenter? Mr Wood from Happy Families. A gossip? Try Blabbo or Miss Drusilla Clack. The dramatist deals them out like a pack of cards, and you can tell at once which is the Queen and which the Knave. Hero, heroine and villain provide the picture cards, and no melodrama is complete without them.

Every manly heart will beat for George, the handsome hero. No one else is so brave, so dashing, so honourable, and so stupid, so utterly devoted to the heroine and so hopelessly incapable of underhand dealing to win her. 'Her name', he confides in *London by Night*,

> whispered hope and comfort to my soul in the dreary watch, the howling storm, the raging battle! When the shots fell like rain, and death stared me in the face at every turn, the thought of her enabled

me to overcome any obstacle, surmount every danger, and secure a fortune which I might lay at her feet.

There is a splash from the Serpentine in *The Lights o' London*: 'George, what are you going to do?' 'Save a life.' He does. A tireless philanthropist ever ready to help the weak, the needy and the oppressed, George is sustained only by the strength of his fists and the protective clichés of his old school tie. 'Muscle, wind, pluck, backbone . . . come where the best man has a chance to win', he ruminates upon the wilds of the Australian bush in *Gold*. Hustled off to a speedy death in *Ruth*, he remonstrates with his captors, 'this forced and secret march, amid storm, and through devious paths, does not appear as if taken in conformity with English law'. Poor George always plays the game, and is taken by surprise when others do not. 'Cowards,' he exclaims in *The Woodman's Hut*,

> do you add insult to your crimes? But tremble, dastards, the day of retribution will arrive! A thousand swords are drawn already to avenge me and inflict a condign punishment on your perfidious master.

This incorrigible optimism is frequently echoed by the lovely Amelia, a heroine who is the blank embodiment of absolute perfection. The bright effulgence of her beauty, which brings strong men to their knees, is equalled only by the unsullied purity of her mind. Magnanimous and unselfish, she is ready to die for her wronged old father in *The Maid and the Magpie*, and in *The Foundling of the Forest* will instantly forgive a penitent villain who for sixteen years has plotted her destruction. If the favoured offspring of luxury and wealth, she rhapsodizes upon the natural world and trips around the castle hamlets distributing jellies to the sick and tracts to the wicked. If translated from rags to riches, she dwells disconsolate in marble halls, begs George not to despise her for possessing a secret fortune of

£20,000, and utters egalitarian sentiments designed to provoke ringing cheers from that mob of nature's gentlemen, the gallery and pit.

With hero and heroine thus assured of an audience's admiration and sympathy the melodramatist is free to build up the threats against them. First on the list comes the villain. Ostensibly driven by ambition, avarice, anger, jealousy or lust to compass George's life, Amelia's chastity or their mutual inheritance, Randall the rotter is most loved by an audience, most wholeheartedly hissed and hated, when endowed with a malevolence more than human, a motiveless malignity which sends shivers of irrational terror down the spine. Such evil provides melodrama with its motor power. Fertile in stratagem and a stranger to scruple, Randall plots, slanders, steals and defrauds with impunity, incites rebellion, hires assassins, murders witnesses, wrecks trains, sinks ships, burns down cottages, blows up banks, and generally does what he can to get the plot moving. When he needs accomplices, a supernumerary crowd of gypsy peddlers, Chinamen, prison warders, decadent Army officers, convicts, bill-pushers and grasping old hags is always on hand. Often he recruits tool villains, who come in two shades: Heartless Black for human bloodhounds, and Cowardly Grey for haggard milksops whose timely defection to virtue materially assists Divine Providence in the last act. Occasionally he joins forces with the villainess, a raven-haired beauty with wicked lips and a succession of sweeping gowns and paste tiaras, who rifles an escritoire for secret despatches in *Dora*, and in *The Derby Winner* vamps the hero, cuts him savagely with a riding whip when he spurns her, knocks back a tumbler of brandy and hurls the glass into the fire crying 'Revenge!' Randall stops at nothing. 'Would you plunder the poor cast-away?' cries George. 'For what am I here?' replies Black Ralph in *The Dream at Sea*. He thrusts into George's path stupendous obstacles to his health, wealth and happiness. Disinherited, ostracized and outlawed, falsely accused of robbery and murder, hunted for his life by assassins, mutineers, red Indians or the police, George spends most of his time wandering in uncouth lands, cast adrift on the open seas or festering in tyrant's dungeons, bandit's caves or prison cells. Decent, dazed and infinitely gullible, he lives in perpetual danger of instant annihilation. He is shot at by a firing squad, hurled over an Alpine precipice, dumped in the Thames, coshed with an iron handle and pushed down a well, placed senseless on the tracks of an underground railway or in the path of a circular saw, harried by bloodthirsty hordes of Indian sepoys or bound to the deadly Upas tree and exposed to its poisonous exhalations.

George thus engaged, Randall can devote his undivided attention to Amelia, whose helpless perfections attract disaster like a magnet. Whether hypnotized, drugged or abducted, auctioned as a coloured slave, accused by the Secret Avengers or arrested for robberies committed by a thieving magpie, threatened with death on mill-race or Channel steamer, locked in a ship's boiler by a jealous lady matador, doped with chloral-impregnated whisky on the upper floor of a burning house, or captured by tomahawk-wielding redskins in *Nick of the Woods* and 'exposed to the merciless fangs of inhuman fiends! who seek to torture and destroy', the hapless Amelia always suffers early and suffers long. In *Masaniello* she is engulfed by a revolution ('Oh! to perish by the brutal hands of the wild raging populace – my soul shrinks from this agony of terror!'), and in *The Dream at Sea* she is unhappily betrothed, married and inefficiently murdered, prematurely incarcerated in the family vault, removed, revived, abducted and finally stranded in a sea-girt cave with the tide coming in and only a corpse for company. Victorian melo-drama is a man's world, and Amelia is but a tender fragile woman, sacrificed to the avarice of match-making guardians, driven from home with a parental curse, abandoned by a weakling husband who squanders the housekeeping on cards and whisky and wild, wild women, ejected by bailiffs from the mortgaged homestead or tenement garret, and left to die in the gutters of the great city 'forsaken and helpless in the cold and pitiless snow' (*Forsaken*). And on every street corner Randall is waiting to renew his lascivious persecutions by flattery, promises, threats or force. 'Helpless and unprotected, with no friend but innocence – no advocates save tears – how will she now repel his violence?' asks *The Castle Spectre*. Incapable of feigning acquiescence until a chance for escape presents itself, Amelia bursts into tears, begs for mercy, threatens suicide, hurls defiance at her persecutors, defends her honour with poignards or a handy wine decanter and, making good her escape from an upper casement, flees for her life, traversing rough country with lightning speed, a child in her arms and frustrated villains in hot pursuit. 'Powers of mercy protect me! How shall I escape these human bloodhounds?' begs Eliza in *Uncle Tom's Cabin*, and floats to safety across the Ohio River on a convenient cake of ice. Enter Amelia from *The Woodman's Hut*, pale and exhausted, her dress torn,

> *her hair in disorder. She runs across the stage.* . . . Oh, heaven, what will become of me? I die with fatigue! Merciful providence, abandon me not! Restore me to safety, or end my sufferings at once. Ah, my pursuers approach! I see them! Whither can I fly – where conceal myself? Ah, a house! (*She runs and knocks.*)

Such obstacles only enrage Randall, who whets his hopes with:

> Her very virtues incense me with a sensuous desire to possess her.
> (*Driven from Home*)
> Curses on the creation! I am sick with torture – and yet (*in a hoarse whisper*) – *she shall be mine*! . . . I will wind like a serpent – I will spring like a tiger – but I will have her! (*Gold*)
> Tomorrow, ah! tomorrow I shall reap my reward! (*Pluck*)

All this omnipotent gloating is supremely overconfident. To-morrow never comes. The exciting climax to Randall's hopes proceeds by well-defined stages. First, the arch denial:

> Do not forget yourself; unhand me, sir, or I will call for help.
> *(Luke the Labourer)*

Second, the attack direct:

> Nay then, proud beauty, you shall know my power – 'tis late – you are unfriended, helpless, and thus – *(he seizes her –* JULIA *screams)*.
> *(The Drunkard)*

And third, the surprising arrival of George for that classic confrontation in which hero, heroine and villain are revealed in their truest colours. To end this section, here are all three of them in pure form from *Adelmorn the Outlaw*:

> BRENNO: Hold! you fly not! That passion burns in my veins, which if you refuse to satisfy, force shall compel.
> INNOGEN: Force!
> BRENNO: Think on your situation –
> INNOGEN: Unhand me –
> BRENNO: You are alone –
> INNOGEN: Monster! –
> BRENNO: Your cries will be unheard –
> INNOGEN: Oh, Heavens! –
> BRENNO: Nay, this struggling –
> INNOGEN: Help, help! Oh, Adelmorn –
> ADELMORN *(rushing from his concealment)*: What shrieks – Villain, desist.

Plot, structure and language are all designed to heighten the persecution inflicted by Randall. The great aim of the plot is to expose distressed innocence to as many trials as possible. Innogen's danger from Brenno in the last extract is extreme, but necessarily of short duration. Another five minutes and perhaps all would be lost. Tie her to the railway track, and the excitement only begins when the express is heard whistling in the wings – and she must be released before it comes thundering past. In melodrama, every crisis generates a suspense so acute it must be resolved at once. But without danger heroes and heroines are without interest. No sooner have they survived one situation, therefore, than the dramatist flings them head-first into another yet more perilous. In *My Poll and My Partner Joe*, George saves a friend from a debtor's prison, is pressganged into the navy on his wedding day, faces a court martial, boards a pirate ship, defeats the villain, storms a fortress and returns home to find his mother dead and his bride married to his partner Joe. There is movement here, but no real progress; a wealth of incident, but a dearth of plot. The structure is episodic. Each situation is more or less self-contained, and the dramatist sweeps us from one thrill to the next without bothering to explain the logical links between them. Often there are none, for when the persecution of innocence is at stake the conventions of melodrama allow plausibility and common sense to be violated with impunity. Twins are always identical, doubles interchangeable and impenetrable disguise can be assumed in seconds – though peasant rags can never hide George's noble blood. To postpone a happy meeting, separated sisters suffer untimely fainting fits or sudden arrest, and both parents of *The Foundling of the Forest* regularly relapse into insensibility, delirium or stark madness whenever the plot threatens a premature family reunion. The 'dead' rise healthily from their graves in *Branded*, and a coward who bursts on stage *'screaming and writhing, with a spear sticking in his back'* makes a perfect recovery by the next scene of *It's Never Too Late to Mend*. Thus fortified, villainy can continue its persecutions indefinitely. And the more flagrantly outrageous these accidents, coincidences and recoveries are, the more paranoiac our sense that the entire universe is in league against the innocent hero. To give these successive dangers 'bite', the dramatist usually makes them more violent and bloodcurdling as the play proceeds. Negro slaves and Christian martyrs are regularly dragged on stage, beaten up, tortured or lynched – and poor George is always threatened with no less. *Gentleman Jack* stages a boxing bout, and in *A Naval Cadet* young Cornell in faultless evening dress is obliged to peel off his white gloves for a protracted punch-up with the villain. Uneven fights with an assortment of daggers, swords, pistols, carving knives and bare fists regularly keep the adrenalin pulsing till the final curtain, and there are buckets of blood in Surrey-side dramas like *Sweeney Todd*, who cries 'I've polished him off!' every time he cuts another throat.

Fast action and plenty of it is the rule, then, and melodrama takes care never to clog the movement with too many words. In my quotation from *Adelmorn the Outlaw*, it is clear that Brenno's threats and Innogen's cries are little more than stage directions for the actors ('Nay, this struggling –'). The scene would make perfect sense to a deaf spectator. Often language serves only to convey unactable information. Melodramatic expositions are brisk and perfunctory, a necessary chore to be finished as soon as possible. 'Draw yourself a chair' says the old man, embarking at once on twenty-five years of potted family history. In *Plot and Passion* the butler and the ladies' maid dust the paper flowers telling each other, for the audience's benefit, what both of them already know. Similarly, changes of heart or plan are speedily conveyed in laconic soliloquy or absurd aside, and the presumed location of a stock setting baldly established by opening the dialogue with 'Welcome, Frank Marchmont, to The Cedars, at Wandsworth' (*London by Night*). Even more succinct are those two plotting villains from *A Tale of Mystery* who divide a sentence between them:

MALVOGLIO: He's coming.
ROMALDI: Let us retire and concert –
MALVOGLIO: Then, at midnight –

c

ROMALDI: When he sleeps –
MALVOGLIO: He'll wake no more! *(Exeunt.)*

Whenever possible, melodrama does away with language altogether, and in many thrilling scenes the action moves so fast that
characters have time only for breathless exclamations. This one,
which is typically incendiary, comes from the climax of *The
Cataract of the Ganges*:

> *The burning trees fall on all sides, and discover the terrific Cataract
> of Gangotri, supposed to form the source of the Ganges – the Emperor
> and the Bramin's troops appear, pouring down the rocky heights
> around the Cataract in every direction – Iran . . . becomes personally
> engaged in combat with two of the Mahomedan Chiefs.*
>
> IRAN: Fly, Zamine, fly! – my steed will bear you safely! – The
> Cataract! – the Cataract! – we have no other hope!
> *Zamine mounts the Courser of Iran, and while he keeps the foe at
> bay, dashes safely up the Cataract, amidst a volley of musketry from
> the Enemy on the heights – the Rajah, Mordaunt, and Robinson
> enter at the head of the combined Mahratta and Jahrejah Army –
> the contest becomes general – horse and foot are engaged in all parts
> . . . Mokarra is killed by a pistol shot from Robinson – Iran brings
> forward Zamine in safety – the Rajah joins their hands – and the
> Curtain falls on the shouts of the Conquerors.*

In short, to sustain Randall's persecutions, the dramatist devises
an episodic plot full of dangerous threats and implausible rescues,
pandering to violence, cutting back the verbiage and rounding
off the whole with a spectacular climax in which even the scenery
joins the conspiracy against virtue triumphant.

The Victorian proscenium-arch was a gigantic picture frame
which melodrama filled with gigantic pictures. Managers spent
huge sums on gorgeous costumes and grandiose scenery. To
create perspective, armies of children marched over distant
mountains and across 'practical' bridges, while adult actors in
the foreground fought stupendous battles with real horses and

drowned in shallow tanks of real water. Elephants, lions and boa-constrictors took the stage by storm. Every act leads up to its 'tableau', where characters 'groupe' or 'form picture' as the curtain descends. The battlefield of *Michael Strogoff* reminded one critic of a plate from the *Illustrated London News* and some-times famous pictures were imitated on the stage. *The Brigand* 'realized' three engravings by Eastlake, and the last act of *The Harbour Lights* rose on 'Picture realized of waiting for the life-boat to come in'. But this pictorialism is more than decorative; as my quotation from *The Cataract of the Ganges* demonstrates, the landscape of melodrama is always designed to persecute the hero, and the physical dangers to which he is exposed are limited only by the ingenuity of the scene-painter and the stage carpenter. Taking more than a hint from *Les Victimes cloîtrées*, 'Monk' Lewis introduced the divided set to the English stage in *Venoni*, where George chips through a dungeon wall 'of immense thick-ness' to rescue Amelia, visible throughout in an adjacent cell. *Jonathan Bradford*'s inn shows two bars downstairs and two bedrooms above, connected by a tile roof *via* which the murderer escapes. To test George's powers of survival to the limit, drama-tists often fling him into a universe ravaged by earthquake, avalanche, fire and flood, all of which required great technical ingenuity. Substantial buildings painted on shallow wooden blocks collapse at the pull of a string, and magnesium strips, red flares and flame-coloured silk agitated by a fan lend plausibility to many incendiary effects. The towers of Montgatz are blown up in *Tékéli*, and a robber's stronghold exploded in *The Miller and his Men*. *Masaniello* shows Vesuvius in eruption, with lava rushing down the mountainside into the sea. Earthquakes destroy an amphitheatre in *The Last Days of Pompeii*, and when a mine is sprung in *The Queen of Cyprus* '*a vast pile of building falls at the back, and discovers the Venetian galleys at anchor, all on fire, with combatants on board*'. Large sections of the floor could be raised or lowered at will, and sometimes replaced with tanks of real water into which smaller tanks installed above the stage poured convincing cascades. Hence *The Cataract of the Ganges* and the 'stupendous Waterfall' of *Rinaldo Rinaldini*, which precipitates itself into a dangerous river navigable, apparently, by gondola. Full-scale ships with all hands on deck rise from the ocean bed in *Carlmilhan* and go down in flames in *The Red Rover*. *Mazeppa* uses the diorama, a vast length of canvas painted with a continuous landscape and wound from one perpendicular roller to another instead of a backcloth. The hero is bound naked to a wild stallion and sent galloping across Poland. Eventually they reach water, and while the horse wades up stream to the left the diorama shows us the entire course of the Dneiper River unwinding to the right. Papier mâché timber-wolves howl on the opposite bank, and when a gigantic vulture descends on wire from the flies even the intrepid Mazeppa loses heart:

> These waters, then, shall be my welcome grave – *(music)* – and see – yon horrid bird of prey, now hovering over its destined victim, forewarns me that my torments soon shall end. – It brings me, too, the sacred consolation that I have reached my native Tartary, to which its form and plumage are peculiar.

Ghosts and visions add even greater horrors. 'Scruto' consists of narrow strips of wood glued onto a canvas loop which is stretched between two rollers like the track of a tank. Fix it to the base of a large trap and the ghost of Louis dei Franchi in *The Corsican Brothers* glides *sideways* as it rises from beneath the stage. Back-cloths of stretched silk and tinted gauze lend mist, fog or even enchantment to any view, and when the new gas lighting is played behind a painted gauze, solid walls dissolve into pink clouds, technicolour sunsets or terrifying visions. *The Flying Dutchman*'s phantom ship appears in the sky '*à la phantasmagorie*', and when the magic bullets are cast in *Der Freischütz* clouds obscure the moon, wheels of fire appear, a skeleton stag is pursued

across the sky by skeleton hounds and skeleton huntsmen, trees
are torn up by the roots and rocks split asunder.

These dangers, threatening George with annihilation or heart-
failure, are the stock-in-trade of melodrama. When they palled,
Boucicault developed the 'sensation' scene, where the combined
talents of carpenter, painter, machinist and property man threw
George and Amelia into even more spectacular jeopardy. As
Ffolliott chisels his way out of prison in *The Shaughraun* ('The
mortar is as soft as butter. This was done by government contract')
the outside wall revolves to show him sneaking through the
orifice and across the prison yard. In *Arrah-na-Pogue* the wall
pivots *and* sinks, allowing Shaun to escape through a window and
climb to freedom up an ivy-girt tower. Boucicault also exposed
Pauvrette to an Alpine avalanche which 'entirely buries the whole
scene to the height of twelve or fifteen feet', and with yards of
crumpled green gauze he transformed the stage floor into open
water for *The Colleen Bawn* to drown in – though with the aid
of a double and some neat trapwork she bobs up all over the stage
and is rescued by the comedian. He blew up a steamer loaded with
cotton and turpentine in *The Octoroon*, burned down a whole-
stage house in *The Poor of New York* and with miniature cut-outs
staged the Boat Race in *Formosa*, and the Derby in *The Flying
Scud*. 'Druriolanus' Harris went one better, using real horses for
the Goodwood Cup in *A Run of Luck* and for the Grand National
in *The Prodigal Daughter*. Because the stage was so confined,
their pace was rather sluggish; and on the first night of *The
Derby Winner* the favourite refused to budge from the starting
post, thereby rendering Virtue destitute and Vice triumphant.
Happily, machinists installed 'scruto' flush with the stage floor,
and the chariot race in *Ben Hur* and the Newmarket meeting in
The Whip went off at full gallop. Meanwhile other sensation
scenes proliferated. *The Sea of Ice* gradually breaks up, waves
are glimpsed, Captain Raoul and Louise sink on separate floes

and their orphan child is left alone amid the dreary bergs, bathed in white light and praying hard. Hero and villain struggle to the death on punts in the Thames in *The Golden Daggers*, in an air balloon over Hampstead Heath in *The Great Ruby* and in diving suits on the seabed in *The White Heather*, where George hacks through Randall's air supply with a dagger. Two villains locked in combat fall out of an airship in *Sealed Orders*, leaving the villainess to be shot down by an anti-aircraft gun. *Deadwood Dick's Last Shot* includes the raising of the American flag by an educated horse. *Under the Gaslight* is the first melodrama to tie innocence to the railway track, and *The Way of the Transgressor* rescues Amelia from this plight with two Landseer dogs, one of which gnaws through her bonds while the other climbs a ladder and alters the signal light with his teeth. At first, one sensation sufficed for each play. Later there was one for every act. *Pluck*, which is described in the prologue as 'a simple story of everyday life', includes a blazing house, the departure of the heroine in a carriage and pair, a mob storming a bank and breaking real glass windows, a 'Grand Snow Storm' which completely covers a numbed and frozen child, a railway crash and the collision of a second train into the wreckage of the first.

All these excitements are increased by background music. Until the repeal of the patent laws in 1843 musical items were obligatory at the minor theatres, and characters in the most painful circumstances regularly burst into barely relevant songs. Several numbers from *Adelmorn the Outlaw* reappear unchanged in *One o'Clock*, and the fisherfolk of *Masaniello* successfully divert suspicion from their revolutionary plans by striking up their favourite barcarole as the guards approach. Even at the major houses choruses of huntsmen, peasants, gypsies, nuns and soldiers lend vocal support to the weddings and funerals of their betters, brass bands boost triumphal processions and minstrels in medieval courts sing jolly glees. Although such divertissements died away as the century advanced, melodrama always lived up to its name. In the great tradition of Holcroft and Rousseau music is used to point character, underline mood and heighten tension. It announces the arrival of every clan in *The Lady of the Rock*. Plaintive heroines flee to *tremolo* violins, bandits with cat-like tread prowl to *pizzicato* strings, and combatants in *The Dumb Maid of Genoa* time every blow with the orchestra, parrying to pirouettes and stabbing each other to strong chords. Chords also emphasize important facts. Everyone gets the message when *The Shade*, pointing to the ruined cloister, cries:

> Blondel – there thy friend was foully murdered! *(music in a terrific chord)* Blood for blood! *(chord more terrific)* Revenge! *(chord)* Revenge! *(chord)* Revenge! *(chord – thunder)*.

Music adds pathos too. When George leaves his beloved Susan in *Gold*, wending his way over the hill in the general direction of Australia, the band plays 'Home sweet home', and as Susan Hopley (in the play of that name) bewails her dead parents '*a flute is heard in imitation of the nightingale*'.

Poor Susan needs this moment of sentimental indulgence. She cannot be forever wringing her hands in despair. The strain would be too much. The agonies of persecuted innocence, brought about by human villainy, heightened by fast-moving and violent action, and reinforced by spectacular scenic dangers and emotive musical accompaniment, demand occasional relief in sympathetic tears or uncomplicated laughter. Melodrama has minor characters designed to serve up both in generous helpings. Good old men sit sorrowing in old-fashioned chairs, like Farmer Wakefield in *Luke the Labourer*:

> Am I not ruined? No farm, no land! Blight, distemper, and misfortune have swept away all, and I am now a bereft and comfortless old man. . . . What have I to look forward to? Nothing but a pauper's life, and then I shall break my heart; and when I be nailed down to be carried to my grave, no one will care, no one will know about it;

there will be no passing bell, nothing to let folks know there goes poor Farmer Wakefield.

Aged parents always bemoan their present miseries, recall the happy days gone by and implore heaven to look with mercy upon their children far away. Widowed mothers die in penury while George is on the high seas ('And I not here to close her eyes!' murmurs the hero of *My Poll and My Partner Joe*, '*staggering*' under the news). White-haired fathers moulder patiently in dungeon cells, cast ruined maidens from their cottage doors, or set off with revolvers, compasses and grandfather's map to save them from the sinful city. And angel children are always infallible tear-jerkers. When Daddy is in prison, Nevada or the public-house they plague the destitute Amelia for blankets, candles and crusts of bread. Occasionally they turn up at the condemned cell to heighten the sorrow of his last earthly moments. Abused, neglected, left to starve, they are at different periods thrown to the lions, buried in snow drifts, locked in punishment jackets or torn from Amelia's arms by a cruel Court Order. Often they fall ill; sometimes they die, like little Lord Fernside in *The Derby Winner*. In *East Lynne*, erring Isabel gains admission to her husband's house as a governess, nurses her sweet and unsuspecting William in this disguise, and falls across the dead body crying 'Oh, Willie, my child! dead, dead, dead! and he never knew me, never called me mother!' But melodrama's most famous angel child is Little Eva in *Uncle Tom's Cabin*, who dies of saintly innocence whispering 'Oh! love! joy! peace!' while the plantation hums with hymns and Daddy sinks to his knees with 'Farewell, beloved child! the bright eternal doors have closed after thee. We shall see thy sweet face no more.' In this, however, he is mistaken, for the play ends with a technicolour apotheosis complete with:

> *Gorgeous clouds, tinted with sunlight.* EVA, *robed in white, is discovered on the back of a milk-white dove, with expanded wings, as*

if just soaring upward. Her hands are extended in benediction over ST CLARE *and* UNCLE TOM, *who are kneeling and gazing up to her. Expressive music – slow curtain.*

After such scenes of heavy pathos, the funny man comes on and entertains the audience with a selection of side-splitting jokes. Melodrama finds no incongruity in this sudden whirligig of emotions. In *The Green Bushes* Miami has no sooner bade farewell to her adulterous lover Connor than Jack Gong appears, to play *Zip Coon* on the fiddle while Grinnidge and Tigertail dance a double hornpipe. Miami then shoots Connor, Grinnidge remarks 'She's settled the settler' and the heroine comes on to weep over the body crying 'Pray, pray let me drag you to the spot where my husband lies weltering in his gore'. Often the comic provides a vulgar commentary upon the main plot. A loyal servant to George and Amelia, he deflates their high-falutin' romanticism by reference to a code of values based on earthy common sense. George can live on love alone, but the funny man needs a pudding in his belly. 'I can't marry another gal,' he complains in *The Harbour Lights*, 'I've got "Peggy" tattoed on my arm'. By voicing our scepticism of the heroic code within the framework of the play itself, he anaesthetizes our disbelief and consequently strengthens our sympathy for George. His chief function, however, is to create hilarious mirth. He enjoys puns of the 'Come to your Mariner's Arms' variety, is sure to hear 'assault and battery' as 'salt and buttery', and has a pretty wit in repartee. 'Your name is Lodowick?' asks Herman in *Adelmorn the Outlaw*. 'Is it? Thank you for the information!' comes the lightning reply. Every joke is a new-minted wonder. 'I never felt so happy since the day my Mother in law was run over by a omnibus' declares Isadore de Montmorency in *The World*. Often the funny man is joined by the funny woman, a pert and lovable soubrette who dances specialities and cuffs his ears. Like the broker's men in the panto-mime, they indulge in witty crosstalk in front of a shallow painted cloth to cover elaborate and noisy scene changes on the main stage. And there is always good fun to be had from the supporting grotesques like the cockney Peter von Bummel who dresses up as a shepherdess in *The Flying Dutchman*, or Miss Spindle in *The Drunkard*, a superannuated spinster who declares, quite truthfully, 'Age cannot wither me, nor custom stale my infinite vacuity.'

Finally, when all these thrills and tears and jokes have been exhausted, dream justice comes into play. In real life, as everyone knows, the evil often flourish like the green bay tree. Art can be more discriminating, and in *The Tragedies of the Last Age* (1677) Thomas Rymer first proposed an ideal 'poetic justice' which punishes the wicked and rewards the virtuous in exact proportion to their deserts. The concept was taken up by Dryden and John Dennis and despite the opposition of Addison in the fortieth *Spectator* (16 April 1711) it rapidly became established as a neo-classical commonplace for the justification of dramatic art on moral grounds. The Georgian stage practised what the critics preached. With prologues advertising their impeccable didacticism, Lillo and Moore sent *The London Merchant* and *The Gamester* to maudlin but moral death as a dreadful warning to others. Mercier, Diderot and Sedaine produced French imitations and adaptations which only slightly softened the trenchant moral tone, and under their influence Pixérécourt at the turn of the century embarked upon some sixty-odd *mélodrames* all demonstrating that the heavens are just, crime never pays and the wages of sin is death. To the Victorian melodramatist such sentiments were unquestioned dogma – and for the very reasons Addison had adduced against them. 'Good and Evil happen alike to all Men on this Side the Grave' he declared, and poetic justice is therefore a falsification of life. The Victorian audience preferred such dreams. Generations bred in the narrow but familiar patterns of village life found themselves alone in a city of strangers, and at the mercy of random and outrageous fortune. The kindly gods of melodrama assured them that chastity was chaperoned by fate, chance could be tamed, and villainy always defeated by a sock on the jaw. A theatre which preached such comforting morality could be patronized with a clear conscience; a ticket for the play was no longer an instant passport to eternal damnation. Moreover, poetic justice permits the free indulgence of our fears. The storms and shipwrecks of melodrama, its inundations, conflagrations, explosions, earthquakes and avalanches, its threats of sudden death by water, poison, rope or steel, its tears and fears and emotional agonies can be savoured in all their terror because we are confident that innocence is indestructible and its ultimate triumph guaranteed. There *are* angels above who favour virtue, and the hour of retribution *will* one day arrive. It is a belief shared by the entire *dramatis personae*, by baffled heroes and persecuted heroines, by Good Old Men and Faithful Servants, by professionals like Friar Austin in *The Count of Narbonne* (who uses it to excuse professional incompetence) and even by the Tartar Khan in *Mazeppa*.

And they are always right. The tide of ill-luck always turns in the last act, the reinforcements always arrive in time, and countless innocents are rescued from death at the eleventh hour by the villain's confession or a timely reprieve. Firing squads shoot at the hero with dummy ammunition, and an army of invading Jahrejahs is converted into cheering allies by a single speech of some dozen or sixteen lines. Unexpected riches are happily discovered, hidden in a waistcoat lining or stuffed in the padding of Granny's old armchair. Vital clues are suddenly unearthed, and if none exist a dream vision gets the dénouement under way. 'Beloved sister!' cries the shade of Andrew to Susan Hopley, 'follow the murderers to the Old Manor House at Upton . . . and confound the guilty in the stronghold of their crimes!' She does just that. Melodrama has an extensive range of such speedy labour-saving devices. Infants stolen from cradles, sold to gypsies or abandoned on the Cathedral steps are regularly endowed with strawberry birthmarks, bottle-green eyes, miniature portraits, lockets of hair, caskets of jewels or superior personal linen by which they are identified twenty years later as the long-lost heirs of vast domains. Lost children adopted by wealthy foster parents can be easily located by singing their favourite carol in the snowy street below. Deep scars inflicted by wolves, daggers or human teeth identify grown men when the time is ripe. And there is always The Call of Blood, by which drunkards, countesses and respectable working girls recognize their immediate family across the chasms of social class. Awful Secrets are always revealed and The Missing Papers found. These necessary documents provide endless excitement. Heroes are always searching for secret despatches, scientific formulae, forgotten marriage-lines, mortgage deeds, holograph confessions or forged receipts, and every villain hides a will of his own. The chase is often circuitous. In *London Pride* important papers are enclosed in a stamped addressed envelope and popped for safe keeping into a pillar-box. The villain recovers them from the slit with a fish-hook. 'This letter', declares the hero of *Pluck*, 'was written by Ellen to me, intercepted by Kean, handed to Clinton, given to George, and left with me. It has had a roundabout journey, but it's here at last to bowl the villains out.' And it always does. At the last moment, friends rally round, Providence smiles, and when all else fails George's honest strength wins the day. Thrown overboard into stormy seas tied in a sack, Dantès lives to revenge his wrongs and claim the treasures of Monte Cristo. *Jack Sheppard*, locked in the condemned hold, breaks his handcuffs with his teeth, twists his fetters asunder, climbs the chimney, hacks through an upper wall into the cell above, smashes down two prison doors, and gaining the roof (''Tis a fearful height') shins to safety down a blanket torn into strips. In the course of *The World* George is exploded, wrecked, shot, chloroformed, certified, locked in a private asylum, chased across the rooftops, attacked with knives, and exposed for 'twenty-three days on a frail raft under a tropical sun – without food and almost without water'. He still survives. George is virtually indestructible, and in the drama's final moments reappears from the dead ('Alive! alive! you alive!' falters the villainess in *Lady Audley's Secret*) to clear the innocent, confound the guilty and collect by curtain-call the fortune, the farmstead and the bride. In the popular melodrama of triumph there is no paltering with poetic justice. Betrayed maidens and erring wives lose their reason, plunge into ravines or die of sin (a fatal disease in melodrama). And when the curtain rises on Waterloo Bridge by moonlight, you may be sure it will not fall until some ruined creature has jumped from the centre span crying:

> I will no longer hesitate – no . . . Merciful Heaven, forgive me! Oh! . . . I shared his sufferings – his wretchedness – whilst he has abandoned me . . . I could bear all but his desertion – forgive him all but that. Pardon, Heaven, that I brave thy anger – one bold step. Oh, Herbert – cruel Herbert! . . . Mother, I come! – I come! – receive thy child in Heaven – one plunge – . . . *(Precipitates herself from the bridge into the river.)*
>
> *(The Scamps of London)*

Even the blackest villains are made painfully aware of their ultimate destination. In *The Murder of the Glen* the accursed Luttrell is shot down from the roof of the Mansion House, and brought bleeding onto the stage to die:

> The terrors of death are on me; a public example. The murderer dies in hideous torment. I, alone, did all; the lowest gulf yawns for me; my heart is scorched in flames; hot irons pierce my marrow; fiends are tearing my heart to atoms; the puddle of the cross-roads will be my grave; a stake driven through my body, and the curses of mankind blast the memory of Luttrell. *(Dies in great agony. An interesting tableaux is formed, and the* CURTAIN DESCENDS.)

Randall always loses. Thwarted when about to possess Amelia or lead her down the aisle, blackmailed and betrayed by accomplices who turn Queen's evidence, baffled by bunglers who kill the wrong man, accidentally shot, stabbed or poisoned, arrested by means of exchange telegraph or an automatic camera (for even mechanical inventions obey the dictates of Providence), tricked into confession by a verbal slip or a psychological bluff, entombed with a corpse, hurled from the Monument, crushed beneath a descending lift or arrested at the Calico Ball disguised as the Sultan of Turkey – no ignominy is too shameful, no death too horrible for Randall the rotter. And as the curtain falls on a last great tableau of villainy exploded amid the huzzas of the virtuous, his decisive defeat panders to the bloodlust of the gallery, confirms their touching faith in Divine Providence, and heightens by contrast the enduring happiness of George and Amelia, through whom the audience experience an eminently satisfying vicarious triumph over the persecuting tyrannies and accidents of their own everyday lives.

VARIATIONS

Between 1800 and 1900 these essential elements of popular melodrama did not change. But not even an uneducated audience will pay good money to see the same play every night for a century. Melodramatists had to invent variations. They incorporated waterfalls, horses, mechanical magpies, human monkeys, donkeys, ducks and performing dogs trained to rescue drowning children, dig up bodies, and sink their fangs into the murderer's padded throat. They ransacked newspapers, novels, poems, old plays, history books and atlases; they cribbed from their colleagues in France, Germany and America; they staged last week's invention, yesterday's catastrophe and this morning's trial at the Old Bailey. Above all, they invented new scenery, new characters and new theatrical effects. By turns, melodrama became gothic, brigandish, exotic, military, naval, domestic, regional, historical, romantic, criminal, urban and plain posh. (Of course my categories overlap.) Gothic melodrama trades in gloomy haunted castles ruled by gloomy haunted tyrants much given to locking up abusive young men in gloomy haunted dungeons below the moat. Luckily there is a secret passage to the ruined cloister of some neighbouring convent, with suits of armour, animated portraits, or skeletons bearing flaming daggers encrusted with blood to point the way. Ghosts and visions are ten a penny. Every night for six months *Adelmorn the Outlaw* hears a phantom voice crying 'Adelmorn, go home'. *The Castle Spectre* turns out to be '*a tall female figure, her white and flowing garments spotted with blood*' who materializes in the oratory while lights blaze, the organ swells and '*a full chorus of female voices chaunt* "Jubilate!"'' Randall, cast as the lascivious tyrant, is visibly shaken. Those folded arms and sombre scowls betray a soul in torment. Hideous dreams afflict him, he suffers prolonged and wholly satisfactory agonies of remorse and dies admitting the invincible power of Divine Justice. Late gothic presents him as a poor man's Faust, who pawns his soul for earthly power and reluctantly appeases his Master by periodic libations of human blood. Haunted castles now give way to dæmons, giants, monsters, water-imps, elves, snakes, dragons, werewolves, vampires, skeleton huntsmen, phantom ships and sinking altars, all appearing in thunder and lightning amid showers of blue fire while the moon turns red. A dramatization of Walpole's novel *The Castle of Otranto* in 1781 led the field, which flourished mightily between 1790 and 1820. Roughly contemporaneous is brigand melodrama, where banditti in floppy hats and dirty boots abduct Amelia from the humble cottage of her poor but honest parents and imprison her in their secret mountain cave. The noble peasant who plans her rescue hides from pursuit in a hollow tree. Amelia escapes across a rickety bridge (which promptly collapses into the ravine), a timely explosion sets the forest ablaze and the robbers are left roasting in picturesque despair. Sometimes it is Randall who is the robber chief, and sometimes George. In *La Forêt périlleuse* and *The Brigands of Calabria* Randall is just another gothic tyrant with a burnt-cork moustache. George plays Robin Hood in *Robert, Chef de brigands* and *Marco Spada*. Ultimately, both roles derive from the Moor brothers in *Die Räuber*. Spectacular panto-mimes like *Aladdin* and an equestrian *Bluebeard* which took £21,000 at Covent Garden in the 1810–11 season gave melodrama a financial interest in Eastern exoticism; titles like *Korastikam Prince of Assassins; or, The Dreaded Harem* appear on the bills. There are genies, djinns and assorted spirits, Brahmin priests, Indian palaces, palanquins, pagodas and in *Thalaba the Destroyer* ostriches make their sensational début on any stage. Equally exotic are those military and nautical dramas commemorating an Empire on which the sun would never set. Napoleon loses *The Battle of Trafalgar* and *The Battle of Waterloo* all over again, Sebastopol and Balaclava fall in the Crimea, Jessie Brown fends off the Indian mutiny and Tommy Atkins wins in the Sudan. In American Civil War plays, George and Amelia are generally on different sides, so that he wins the battles and she wins a hero. If peace broke out, history was plundered for *The Fall of Badajoz* or *The Battle of Agincourt*. Whatever the period, there were parades and manœuvres, charges, assaults and pitched battles involving cannon, smoke and firecrackers. Horses reared, forts fell, ships sank, and while the officers behaved like gentlemen jolly tars and tommies routed the tyrant wogs. Lurching through the gun-smoke is melodrama's first working-class hero, Sailor George. A cutlass in each hand and a brace of pistols in his belt, he disposes effortlessly of national foes, wreckers, smugglers and piratical swabs in black wigs and petticoats – all for the sake of England and his Sal whom he regularly describes as a trim little frigate. With his nautical metaphors, patriotic speeches, sea-shanties, hornpipes, baccy box, rum ration, pigtail and quid, Sailor George established in the 1830s an enduring taste for heroes who are ordinary men in the toils of everyday life. In village plays like *The Rent Day* and *Frank the Ploughman* cruel stewards squeeze ruinous rents from the downtrodden peasantry, lawyers named Pounce, Claws, Cribbs, Snapfee and Mucklethrift foreclose mortgages, the old man is imprisoned for debt and his beauteous daughter abducted by Squire Randall in a black frock coat and whiskers. *Rosina Meadows*, being American, tangles with a City slicker instead. Sometimes agricultural depression drives George to the town, where he is victimized by rich mill-owners, replaced by steam-looms or seduced by villains into *The Factory Strike; or, Want, Crime and Retribution*. Lured to London, he surrenders to gambling, wenching or the bottle, which leaves Amelia destitute and George delirious until a passing philanthropist offers him the pledge. 'Louisa,' he vows in *The Drunkard's Warning*, 'hear me while I swear ne'er again to pollute my lips with that accursed fluid that has brought this misery upon us both!'

Less harrowing but far more picturesque are those plays set in regions or periods remote from modern life. *The Lady of the Rock* is Highland gothic, all 'piebrachs' and gathering clans. Others visit the Irish lakes or the Australian goldfields. *Nick of the Woods* belongs to the American frontier, with pork bissings to eat, Shawnee wigwams to burn and that irrepressible buck-tail Ralph Stackpole the ring-tailed squealer to tote the angeliferous Edith over the falls in his canoe. *The Ladye of Lambythe* is about as medieval as its title, but *Richard Plantagenet* has Wat Tyler's revolt, and while *Jack Sheppard* the highwayman is in Newgate – the date is 1724 – Hogarth paints him for 'The Idle Apprentice' and John Gay dreams up *The Beggar's Opera*. In the French version, George I comes on with a royal pardon. Even more glamorous are romantic fancy-dress dramas introducing that perfervid heart-throb, the cape and sword hero. *Don César* began life as the Falstaffian buffoon who tumbles down a chimney in Act Four of Hugo's *Ruy Blas*. In his own play, he is a duellist, poet, wit, raconteur, lover and fearless man of action who survives a firing squad, assaults a hunting lodge amid a volley of musketry, spits the villain and saves the honour of his Queen. Melodrama's greatest swashbuckler, he was followed on stage by *Les Trois Mousquetaires*, *Rupert of Hentzau* and many another Ruritanian sword-and-caper man.

Most melodramas involve crime. Some specialize in it, drawing on real life for the disguises of *Vidocq, the French Police Spy*, the intrigues of Fouché's *Secret Service* or the daring escapes of *Latude*. At the minor houses, recent murders were staple fare. The Surrey staged the Thurtell and Weare case as *The Gamblers*, using the murderers' actual sofa, chair and carriage in the performance, and the Royal Victoria did so many *Maria Martens* and *Sweeney Todds* it became known as the 'Bleedin' Vic'. In *The Ticket-of-Leave Man* George is a blackmailed ex-convict, and in *The Silver King* falsely thinks himself a murderer. Both are resolved by that wonderful invention the Scotland Yard detective, and both include realistic panoramas of metropolitan depravity. Plays like *Les Mystères de Paris*, *The Poor of New York* and *The Great World of London* offer little else. We visit cafés, tea-gardens, railway termini, a silver hell, Blackfriars Bridge, Rat's Castle, Wall Street, quarries near Montmartre, brick-fields in Battersea, the Terpsichorean Saloon, Black Brake Wharf and Cora Fay's gaming house. All human life is here: actors, porters, policemen, costermongers, river rats, grisettes, stockbrokers, cadgers, epileptics, hawkers, peddlers, dram drinkers and drabs. Randall is a cut above them all. Cool, witty and urbane, he dines with dukes, cracks safes in evening dress and boozes till dawn with his cronies in the Mile End Road. Effortlessly, he glides into posh melodrama, where everyone is titled, commissioned, or wealthy to excess. *The Derby Winner* is simply Oscar Wilde with horses. Randall is a major, George an earl, and the Duchess of Milford provides the comic relief. The action moves from a regimental ball to the Royal Courts of Justice, Tattersall's and Ascot. Everyone has five or six changes of costume, and the handprops run to brandy balloons, field glasses and silver salvers. Even in Mayfair, however, virtue still triumphs over the gilded depravity of everyday life. Whatever the setting, popular melodrama preserves its dream intact.

DEVELOPMENTS

In the second half of the century melodrama had more serious changes to face. Popular audiences demanded more and yet more sensation scenes, and a mediocre script was often saved by a good train crash, snowstorm, buzz-saw rescue or Derby Day in each act. Realism became the rage. When he needed a tenement room for *The Easiest Way*, Belasco stripped a real slum of its doors, windows and even wallpaper. At first, this painstaking fidelity lent melodrama an added force: the Providence which halts a convincing express train inches from Amelia's neck must indeed be Divine. Other developments were less constructive. Smaller, more comfortable theatres began to attract a polite, literate audience with a taste for serious plays with small casts, drawing-room settings, wordy dialogue and 'strong' emotional situations. The ever-popular *Lady of Lyons* deals with a romantic misalliance, *The Moonstone* is a detective drama and *Dora* a spy story set in High Society. These middle-class dramas had a double effect upon the popular melodrama of triumph: they refined its acting style, and softened its moral tone. In urban and posh drama, actors like Du Maurier and Gillette no longer gestured like windmills and ranted like madmen. They dressed quietly, spoke naturally and developed a casual, throwaway technique. E. S. Willard perfected a chilling, unstagey villain in *Romany Rye*, and when George loses £32,000 on the turn of a card in *The Winning Hand*, he acts with 'a nervous, subdued force'. Ringing denunciations of tyranny are now out of place; so too are the naïve triumphs of unblemished virtue. Heroes are executed, villains redeemed and ruined maids dismissed to lasting bliss. Of course, George is always ready to mount the scaffold for his friends. When Sydney Carton does so in *The Only Way*, the first rays of the rising sun light up his face. 'It is', he says, 'a far better thing that I do, than I have ever done. It is a far better rest that I go to than I have ever known' – but this time there is no last-minute reprieve. Other heroes with the Carton complex are Robert Landry in *The Dead Heart*, Lesurques in *Le Courrier de Lyon* (who is sometimes executed for the crimes of Dubosc and sometimes not), and Marcus Superbus in *The Sign of the Cross*, an instantaneous convert to Christianity who meets the lions with Mercia on his arm crying 'Thus, hand in hand, we go to our bridal. Christus hath triumphed! The Light hath come. Come, my bride! Come – to the Light beyond!' Magdalens have always created problems of sympathy in popular melodrama, where unrequited love is a dangerous disease and sin (as we have seen) officially fatal. At the Adelphi in the 1840s, heart-broken gypsy maidens and wild flowers of Mexico or the prairie regularly turn the assassin's dagger to their own bosoms, or intercept the bullet meant for George. Later, death is no longer necessary, and betrayed virgins who leap from cliffs or bridges are sure to find George sculling about in the water below. Finally, sin could even be forgotten and redeemed. In Society plays like *Odette* even the blackmailing adventuress is permitted an act of noble self-sacrifice to save her daughter's marriage, and Mrs Erlynne does as much in *Lady Windermere's Fan*, restoring the eloping heroine to her unsuspecting husband with virtue and even reputation still intact. *The New Magdalen* is redeemed to happiness by the hero of her choice, a penitent whore in *The Two Orphans* completes her rehabilitation by getting herself transported to Guiana in place of the heroine, and in *Tommy Atkins* an unmarried mother works off her guilt by touring the trouble spots of Europe as a Red Cross nurse and is rewarded with marriage to the hearty young curate she really loved all the time. Erring wives are now restored to forgiving husbands in scenes of orgiastic self-pity modelled on the climax of Kotzebue's *Menschenhass und Reue*, translated here by Benjamin Thompson as *The Stranger*:

STRANGER: Farewell!
MRS HALLER: A last farewell! . . .
> *Their hands lie in each other; their eyes mournfully meet each other. They stammer another 'Farewell' and part; but as they are going she encounters the boy and he the girl.*
CHILDREN: Dear father! Dear mother!
> *They press the children in their arms with speechless affection; then tear themselves away, gaze at each other, spread their arms, and rush into an embrace. The children run and cling round their parents. The curtain falls.*

Penitent villains are as morally subversive as magdalens and much more common. At the show-down of *Deaf and Dumb*, the usurping uncle bursts into tears, promises restitution, and is saved from public disgrace by the Good Old Man. This is the palliative tradition of *drame*. Equally powerful is the notorious 'double standard' of Victorian morality, which allows a young man to sow his wild oats but punishes with death any girl who steps a foot from the narrowest path of righteousness. In *Masaniello*, Fenella plunges into a sea of molten lava, but her remorseful ravisher is offered lasting happiness with the enchanting heroine. Highwaymen and housebreakers like *Paul Clifford* and *Cartouche* usually pay the price of sin and crime, but their penitent speeches on the scaffold proved so inadequate a counterblast to three acts of glamorous adventure that in the 1860s the Lord Chamberlain had to banish them from the stage. In the next decade, sympathetic criminals reappeared at the Lyceum, where Irving's great art transformed a clutch of cliché villains into remorseful, haunted heroes. His Flying Dutchman became another Faustus, and Mathias in *The Bells*, Macbeth. Mathias is an unsuspected murderer who dreams he is forced to re-enact his crime before a court of justice which sentences him to hang; staggering from his bed next morning he gasps 'The rope! the rope! Cut the rope!' and falls dead. Talien played him in *Le Juif polonais* as an earthy, cunning rogue whose harrowing end reaffirms Divine Justice. Irving made him a good man tortured to death by an unbearable conscience. It is an interpretation which leads directly to the psychotic murderers of modern thrillers like *Rope*, *Gaslight* and *Night Must Fall*. When villains are pitiable delinquents, and Divine Retribution leads directly to the psychologist's couch, melodrama is dead.

By 1918, melodrama on the stage was virtually extinct. There were several causes. The new style of realistic low-keyed acting had no time for high-flown rhetoric and large effects: when Du Maurier revived *Diplomacy* in 1913 he cut out all the 'big' speeches. An exciting new toy called the cinema showed sensation scenes with a realism beyond the stage carpenter's wildest dreams. Freud's insights into the complexities of human motivation made George and Amelia look rather foolish, and after the horrors of the First World War it was difficult to believe in poetic justice any more. The old stock companies gave way to glossy touring productions sent out from London and New York, and melodrama's traditional repertory disappeared from the boards. Metropolitan houses catering to the carriage trade sold out to the problem play and the murder mystery. Ibsen and Shaw shocked the intellectuals and the popular audiences took themselves off to the Music Hall, the Buffalo Bill Roadshow, and the heartless horrors of the Grand Guignol. Melodrama retreated to the friendly theatres of the East End and the Bowery (the Boulevard had already passed away), and then took to the road. For ten, twenty or thirty cents shopgirls from Seattle to Savannah could see *Nellie, the Beautiful Cloak Model* or *The Chinatown Trunk Mystery*, tricked out with burning houses, sinking battleships, detectives, comedians, animals and slinking Oriental despots. One or two new plays conceived in the old style became fashionable freaks. *The Green Goddess*, which began a London run of 416 performances in 1923, is an exotic throwback, complete with Himalayan temples, a lascivious but sophisticated Raja and a persecuted heroine saved from death or dishonour by the last-minute arrival of the Royal Air Force. 'We must keep a stiff upper lip, and play the game' says George, without a trace of self-parody. Equally innocent is *Young England*, in which a plucky guidemistress and a villainous scoutmaster tussle over blueprints for the new Town Hall. It achieved 278 unintentionally hilarious performances in 1934, before the Lord Chamberlain withdrew its licence as a risk to the peace. Finally, a revival of *The Drunkard* at the Theatre Mart, Los Angeles, which opened in 1933 and ran for twenty-six years. With 9,477 performances, it holds the record for the longest-running play in the world. It is but a step from this to Bruce Brandon's 'old-fashioned mellow-drama' *On the Bridge at Midnight*, and Brian J. Burton's pastiche versions of *East Lynne* and *Lady Audley's Secret*, which some amateur dramatic societies and rugger clubs find so entertaining.

Yet obsequies are out of place. The melodrama of triumph still flourishes on the modern stage, in the protest plays discussed in Chapter 4 or in disguised form as classical opera and ballet. For when mime and music replace the tedious spoken word, the most sophisticated audience seems ready to accept the simplified characters, impossible plots, scenic marvels and cosy poetic justice of this conventionalized dream world. Tchaikovsky's ballet scores are rich in thunder claps and showers of fire and beautiful princesses persecuted to strong 'chords'. Bouilly's *Léonore* gave Beethoven the text for *Fidelio*, which is melodrama in more than the musician's sense. Noble Florestan rots in Pizarro's dungeon, Leonora risks her life to save him, a trumpet call announces the timely arrival of rescuing troops, and Pizarro is punished and Florestan freed amid universal joy. Wagner, Verdi and Puccini still pack Covent Garden and La Scala for operas built upon the most successful melodramas of their day.

Then again, popular audiences found the tired clichés of stage melodrama new-minted marvels on the silver screen. Rapid cross-cutting allowed for instantaneous scene-changes and while Amelia mimed elaborate distress a pit pianola tinkled through 'Hearts and Flowers' or the hurry music from *William Tell*. Trick photography showed dissolving ghosts and ice-floes sinking with a realism far beyond the derisory cardboard splendours of the stage. 'It will be the real thing in every respect' boasted Vitagraph of *Uncle Tom's Cabin*, 'real ice, real bloodhounds, real negroes, real actors, real scenes from real life as it really was in the antebellum days!' Bernhardt filmed *La Dame aux camélias* as *Camille*, James O'Neill played *The Count of Monte Cristo* yet again, and Anna Pavlowa danced *The Dumb Girl of Portici*. As the supply of stage classics dried up, serial cliff-hangers began. *The Perils of Pauline* exposed Pearl White to a new catastrophe at the end of every reel. 'The action of the story' declared a press release 'includes flying machine accidents, thrilling rescues, fires at sea, train wrecks, automobile accidents, in fact, everything that can be introduced as a thrill.' And the enterprising Miss White, scorning an understudy, performed them all herself. Since then, most of melodrama's stock ingredients have appeared on the screen. Doggy dramas like *Le Chien de Montargis* littered Lassie, Strongheart and Rin-Tin-Tin. Gothic melodrama established Boris Karloff as the definitive monster in *Frankenstein*, and then moved on to dinosaurs, man-sized ants, *Planet of the Apes* and *2001*. *The Battle of Agincourt* was remade as *The Battle of Britain*. Errol Flynn glamorized *The Adventures of Robin Hood* and the Douglas Fairbankses swashbuckled through various musketeers. Picturesque robbers reappear in *The League of Gentlemen* (in which a mess of army officers raid a bank), Edward G. Robinson transplants urban crime to gangster-ridden Chicago in *Little Caesar*, and *Ten Rillington Place* surpasses even the blood-boltered horrors of *Sweeney Todd*. *Psycho* derives its suspense and thrills from a mentally disturbed murderer. Biblical epics like *Quo Vadis?* add only Hollywood spectacle to the trusty formula of sadism, sex and salvation made popular in *The Sign of the Cross*. The rags-to-riches story hinted at in *Pauvrette* achieves full-blown expression in those glossy bio-pics where struggling scientists and composers fight off poverty, prejudice and public indifference, and in the last reel announce to an applauding world the discovery of radio, radium or some deathless melody. An inbred variation is the self-regardant show-biz biography of *Star* or *The Glenn Miller Story*. But the cinema's greatest melodrama is the western, where moral judgments are as clear-cut as a gunman against the skyline, ambushed mails, detonated mines and rescuing cavalry provide the thrills, and John Wayne walks down that long, deserted main street at high noon to fight it out with Injuns, cattle thieves or crooks. In the old days of Tom Mix and William S. Hart, when men were men and women were children, virtue always won; nowadays romance rides the range, critics talk of mythic meanings and nothing is certain any more. Television at least preserves the proprieties in *The Virginian*, and develops its own brand of criminal melodrama in those police court and private-eye serials where armies of incorruptible attorneys, detectives, coppers and hired guns wage ceaseless war against underworld thugs, international spy rings, beautiful vamps and graft in high places. Currently visible are *A Man Called Ironside*,

Softly, Softly: Task Force, Dixon of Dock Green, Z Cars, The Untouchables, The Persuaders! and *Jason King.* Children absorb the same conventions in science-fiction fantasies like *Stingray, Star Trek* and *Dr Who.* When these titles lose their gloss, there will be others. Even today, it seems, we need to slump into armchairs, turn on the box, and escape into a mindless world of indestructible supermen, emotional thrills and triumphant endings. Melodrama, said the *Theatrical Inquisitor* in 1818, appeals to those who 'wish to be amused without the slightest exertion on their own parts, or any exercise whatever of their intellectual powers' (p. 160). Times have not changed.

A DEFENCE

Finally, a word of defence. The Victorian melodrama of triumph dominated the theatres of Europe and America for over a century; on the basis of bulk alone it cannot be ignored. It produced many excellent plays, some of which still hold on the modern stage. In 1968, for example, serious revivals of *The Bells* and *The Shaughraun* appeared in the West End, and the Liverpool Playhouse reopened with *The Lyons Mail.* Melodrama was part of a truly popular theatre. It shows us what life was really like in the navy, on the farm, out of work or down the mine. It charts working-class attitudes to pressgangs, prostitution, alcoholism, rack-rent landlords and colonial expansion. It examines the impact on society of steam looms, iron ships, railways, telegraph systems, wireless, airships, balloons, submarines, imperialist wars and the gold fever which opened up the American frontier and the Australian bush. Today, we have no genuinely popular theatre for the instantaneous discussion of moon landings, prison riots, pollution, apartheid, unemployment, the Common Market, or wars in Vietnam, Northern Ireland and Bangladesh. And we are the poorer for it. Historians in the next century will find

Z Cars or *Cathy, Come Home* a very poor substitute for the richness and vitality of Victorian melodrama.

'But historical value does not guarantee intrinsic merit' say the scholars. 'Melodrama falsifies life, its characters are puppets, its action absurd, its scenic marvels mere theatrical effects, its language grotesque and exaggerated, its poetic justice naïve and its escapism infantile.' True. Art always 'falsifies' life, for every artist selects, arranges and distorts the material of experience until it reflects his own private vision. Even a snap-shot has four edges, which limit the total panorama available to the naked eye. Of course melodrama simplifies character: so do Plautus and Jonson and Molière and Feydeau and Shaw. The *commedia dell'arte* is built exclusively on broad stereotypes, and so are morality plays like *Everyman*. Some dramatic kinds need these blank outlines of innocence and villainy to do their job, and it seems invidious to condemn melodrama for a legitimate practice accepted without question in satire, farce and morality. Besides, a stage character interests us initially not because he is complex, but because he has superabundant theatrical vitality: hence Harpagon, Harlequin and the frenzied energy of George and Amelia, who live every moment of their stage lives at what Hopkins calls 'the highest pitch of stress'. Such roles may read flatly, but the dramatist knows that in performance an actor will endow them with enough of his own physical personality to make them credible; great actors like Irving relished the opportunity they afforded for brilliant displays of theatrical temperament, and Stanislavski used an improvisation of *The Two Orphans* to teach the performers of the Moscow Art Theatre the value of physical action in the theatre. To be sure, melodramatic plotting depends upon outrageous coincidence, impenetrable disguise and impossible changes of heart. But so do *Oedipus Rex*, *The Merchant of Venice* and *King Lear*. Melodrama has no monopoly of such useful conventions, which heighten George's paranoiac sense that all occasions are conspiring against him. Melodrama's much-abused scenic marvels serve the same function. The aim, always, is triumph; to achieve it the dramatist must fling George and Amelia into every conceivable kind of distress. Randall's diabolical villainy, the mindless persecutions of coincidence and chance, the shipwrecks and conflagrations of the natural world – all combine to create a universe of terrifying hostility. Only when George and Amelia have overcome such apparently insuperable obstacles to their health and happiness can the *catharsis* of triumphant melodrama be attained. These apparent absurdities, then, are not the visible signs of a debilitated imagination or a starved technique. They are severely functional and organic. Without them, melodrama could not flourish. Without them, indeed, melodrama could not exist. And if they depend occasionally upon the theatrical effects of a great actor, scene painter or stage carpenter, that is entirely as it should be. To condemn melodrama for being 'theatrical' is as sensible as condemning a painter for using paint.

I should like to press these theatrical values further. Shorn of actors, costumes, scenery, lighting, the rhythms of performance and the moment-to-moment excitement of an audience which *assists* in the French sense at the show, the printed texts of melodrama inevitably look rather thin. Like modern television serials, they were written at incredible speed often for despicable returns. Dibdin browsed through *The Heart of Midlothian* on New Year's Eve, 1818, and had his dramatization on the boards by 13 January. Boucicault took one more day over *The Colleen Bawn*, but then he also chose the scenery, found the music, rehearsed the cast and played the lead. The results may not adorn anthologies of deathless prose, but they do have an admirable vitality and concreteness. The low-life characters of Victorian melodrama speak a Dickensian lingo based on nautical, regional or underworld slang, and they draw their vigorous imagery from everyday life. 'Why, the sky looks as black as the seams of a hackney clerk's

Sunday coat, just rubb'd over with its Saturday night's ink' declares *The Flying Dutchman*. The lofty rhetoric of melodrama's heroes has the same pungency and force. Compare Wilfred Denver's agonized cry in *The Silver King*:

> Oh God! put back Thy universe, and give me yesterday!

with this more sustained passage:

> O God, O God, if I could return to yesterday
> Before I thought that I had made a decision.
> What devil left the door on the latch
> For these doubts to enter? And then you came back, you
> The angel of destruction – just as I felt sure.
> In a moment, at your touch, there is nothing but ruin.
> O God, what have I done?

But this hero does not exit into a snowstorm. He is Edward Chamberlayne in T. S. Eliot's modern-dress comedy *The Cocktail Party*. Melodrama never betrays Eliot's insecurity of tone. It is always grand, when some grand occasion is presented to it. When George defends Madge Wildfire from an angry mob in Dibdin's *The Heart of Midlothian*, he sweeps into unconscious blank verse, as my re-lineation shows:

> I'm known to some of ye – have been your friend,
> Would die defending your just rights; but he
> Who steps a foot beyond this sacred bound
> To trample on affliction and distress,
> Shall through my heart-strings cut his hellish path,
> Or pay the fell intention with his blood.

No doubt this is merely inflated emotional rhetoric, calling for an exaggerated style of delivery. Yet in the circumstances ordinary conversational prose would obviously be incongruous, inadequate and anticlimactic. The characters and situations of melodrama are so extreme and exaggerated that only extreme and exaggerated styles of writing and declamation will do them justice.

Today, this grand style has been lost. Dramatists who attempt it look ridiculous, as the mawkish extract from *The Cocktail Party* shows. And actors who are faced with large-scale emotional rhetoric in revivals of classical plays either pretend they are speaking colloquial prose (like Marlon Brando in the film of *Julius Caesar*), or courageously risk the accusation of 'ham' (like Laurence Olivier in the film of *Othello*). But there are occasions when nothing else will do; even in Shakespeare there are times when nothing succeeds like excess.

'But the facile optimism of melodramatic triumph weakens our moral fibre' say the scholars; 'it invites us to expect the impossible of life, and seriously reduces our capacity to deal with the problems of the real world.' I disagree. We only expect the impossible of life if we assume that the real world is run on melodramatic principles. Every fool can see that it is not, and melodrama does not pretend that it is. To be sure, it copies the surface of reality with minute exactness, but that is only part of the fun. Victorian audiences were not taken in by those mighty cataracts and sleazy slums. What they admired was the skill and ingenuity of the illusion, just as they admired plays like *The Corsican Brothers* and *Vidocq, the French Police Spy* where one actor plays identical twins or assumes a series of lightning disguises. Television addicts today are no less discerning, although the illusion of reality is complete. Eliot Ness and Captain Kirk can brush aside bullets like confetti, but we would not choose to run such risks. We may share their moral principles, but we do not assume that we also share their charmed lives. No one really believes that virtue is impregnable, but from time to time everyone needs to pretend that he does. The dream world of melodrama caters to that need. It posits ideals of courage, integrity, patriotism and moral excellence. It takes the problems of real life, and provides them with model solutions. It dramatizes the fears and threats which oppress us, and reduces them to a comforting emotional pattern.

It gives us the courage and confidence to go on living. And if we reject this triumphant *catharsis* in our waking lives, we may be sure the dream world of melodrama will return to haunt us in our dreams. In a terrifying surrealistic universe of our own manufacture (rather like Orwell's dreaded Room 101) we fight the day's battles all over again; we rant and rave and flee for our lives and overcome villains in deadly combat. The night before a journey, we dream of missing papers and stolen luggage, of trains that crash and aeroplanes that plummet to the sea. Next day, our fears are exorcized and the journey passes off without mishap. In *The Life of the Drama* (1965), Eric Bentley observes '*Melodrama is the Naturalism of the dream life*' (p. 205). Psychologists have shown us that we cannot live without our dreams; it is about time the scholars woke up to the fact that we cannot live without melodrama either. Sometimes, of course, the dream becomes a nightmare and we do not win. The melodrama of triumph reflects only one aspect of our inner lives. There is also the melodrama of defeat. But this is a large topic, and deserves a chapter to itself.

3
Defeat

Two lovers on their wedding day are fooling with a pistol which they think unloaded. Playfully, the groom directs it at his bride and pulls the trigger and shoots her dead. He sends a letter of condolence to her father and falls upon his sword. A loving wife eagerly awaiting her husband's return from overseas is walking by the seashore when his sodden corpse is washed up at her feet. She faints across the body and is 'gone for ever'. Steele tells these stories in *The Tatler* (18 October 1709) to suggest that human miseries are most affecting when they encompass sympathetic innocents who have done nothing to deserve them. This is the essence of the melodrama of defeat. Once again a blameless hero fights against external forces but this time they succeed and he goes under, leaving an audience to pity his distresses or admire the fortitude with which he bears them.

Plays tailored to this pattern may be met in every period, but in the eighteenth century the cult of sensibility enabled them to dominate the stage. Sentimentalists like Steele and Shaftesbury denied the Hobbesian belief that man is an imperfect creature governed by self-interest, and championed instead an optimistic faith in his innate capacity for wishing others well; all virtuous action was the spontaneous expression of this emotional benevolence, and the capacity to shed a sympathetic tear for the miseries of others a certain proof of a refined and virtuous heart. 'By awakening the heart to tenderness,' said William Mudford in his *Life of Richard Cumberland* (1812), 'we can dispose it to the admission of moral truth' (I. 281). And Steele had justified his *Tatler* anecdotes a hundred years before on these same grounds. 'The contemplation of distresses of this sort', he wrote,

> softens the mind of man, and makes the heart better. It extinguishes the seed of envy and ill-will towards mankind, corrects the pride of prosperity, and beats down all that fierceness and insolence which are apt to get into the minds of the daring and fortunate.

Obedient to this mind-softening philosophy, the sentimental dramatist filled his stage with perfect people and flooded them with undeserved misfortune. In comedies like Cumberland's *The Fashionable Lover*, he gave Pixerécourt the plot devices, characters and happy endings of the melodrama of triumph; his serious plays are maudlin melodramas of defeat which measure their success by the bucketsful of tears they can evoke for innocence distressed. With such a criterion of excellence to guide them, it is no marvel Otway, Southerne, Rowe and Lillo wrote the plays they did.

Their settings range from palaces in present-day Bohemia to Caledonian castles in the Middle Ages, but there is no pretence at local colour; in these plays Elizabethan Cornwall is conveyed by a single reference to the brave Sir Walter Raleigh newly arrived at Plymouth from Guiana. The protagonist of eighteenth-century melodrama, thus denied the scenic terrors with which his Victorian descendant will contend, makes up for the deficiency by the intensity of his emotional distress. Take, for example, Southerne's Isabella in *The Fatal Marriage*. We learn that several years before the play begins Biron, her reckless husband, has run through his small allowance and perished at the siege of Candy. In the first act his father, deaf to charity, locks the palace gates against the weeping widow and her pathetic little son. The second act shows her beset by creditors who come to plunder all she has. Next, she is rescued by reluctant marriage to a faithful friend only to be confronted with the reappearance of her former husband ('*He goes to her; she shrieks, and falls into a swoon*').

E

Driven intermittently insane by this unknowing bigamy, she makes a mad attempt on Biron's life, but recognizes him in time and bursts into a flood of self-recrimination. Of course she tries to kill herself, and of course she is prevented. When Biron is done to death by ruffians, she regains her senses long enough to throw herself upon the body, and then goes mad again in time to drag it off. Naturally, her little son is terrified, and runs away from his distracted and dishevelled mother. Eventually she stabs herself, and dies in saintly sanity surrounded by a knot of sorrowing survivors who applaud her 'most injur'd Innocence'. Agonies no less protracted afflict Otway's Monimia in *The Orphan*, who on her wedding night unwittingly gives up her honour to her husband's lustful twin; after wallowing in oceans of remorseful tears, all three seek suicide by dagger, sword or poison. In Lillo's *Fatal Curiosity*, noble Young Wilmot comes home incognito after seven years abroad and is immediately murdered for his money by his parents; they kill themselves upon discovering what they have done.

The essential features of the sentimental melodrama of defeat are clearly visible in this brief sampling of the form. All three plays present an innocent protagonist whose everlasting goodness is the theme of every tongue. And all admit an element of human villainy in bringing these bright angels to destruction. Biron is killed by Carlos, his ambitious younger brother, who had concealed from Isabella knowledge of her husband's life; Monimia is deflowered by Polydore; and Wilmot murdered by his father. But sentimental faith in the innate perfectibility of man encourages the dramatist to find excuses for such wickedness. The Wilmots' crime is palliated by their extreme poverty: 'not choice,/But dire necessity' compels the murder of their unknown guest. And such ignorance effectively diminishes the villain's moral guilt. Like Wilmot *père*, Lord Randolph does not know that Norval is his step-son when he slays him in Home's *Douglas*, and when

Polydore sleeps with Monimia he does not suspect that she is married. When Otway's drama was rewritten as *The Rival Brothers*, Horatio replaces Theodor hoping that Victoria will thus be compelled to marry him to save her honour; he is as horrified as Polydore to learn that what he took for honest fornication was really incest with his brother's wife. Such characters demand forgiveness because they do not know what they are doing. And with the darker stains of human villainy thus bleached away, the dramatist is free to blame the death of innocence on those convenient abstractions, fate and chance. It is the merest accident Biron does not arrive in time to stop his wife's re-marriage, or Castalio to anticipate the lustful Polydore, or Wilmot's true-love to prevent his parents' murderous intent. Barely a moment separates the melodrama of defeat from that of triumph. Indeed, in all these plays, so much depends on accident and ignorance, misunderstanding and mis-timing, that the protagonists seem wholly justified when they complain they are proscribed by some malignant deity.

> The rugged hand of Fate has got between
> Our meeting Hearts, and thrusts 'em from their Joys,

cries Isabella in *The Fatal Marriage*, and Southerne's title openly confirms her fear that the catastrophe is both deadly and predestined. It is the only view he can adopt. A faultless hero cannot bring about his own destruction, and since all human villainy directly contradicts the sentimental ethic, defeat must spring from those superhuman forces whose effects insurance companies term acts of God and atheists dismiss as rotten luck. No teasing problems of responsibility or moral guilt now remain to stem the flow of sympathetic tears for innocence oppressed. 'When I am dead, forgive and pity me' pleads Isabella, and a century-long chorus of deserted maidens, murdered sons and widowed wives takes up the same refrain, from Otway's heroine in 1680 ('Who on Earth/Is there so wretched as Monimia?') down to Jephson's distracted mother in *The Count of Narbonne* of 1781:

> These pangs, these struggles, let them be my last;
> Release thy poor, afflicted, suffering creature;
> Take me from misery, too sharp to bear,
> And join me to my child! *(Falls on the body of* ADELAIDE*)*

In the clear light of common sense such sentimental wallowing in grief is no doubt exaggerated, false, ridiculous and morally unsound; plays which deal exclusively in easy tears, and assume that moral weakness, sin and folly are to be charitably excused, may indeed soften the mind but it is difficult to see how they can improve the moral workings of the heart. And yet psychologists might argue that they satisfy a human need far more vital than that which Steele proposed. These plays do more than beg an audience to surrender to the irresponsible and enervating pleasure of a really good cry; our pity for the protagonist with whom we are identified merges swiftly into pity for ourselves. Self-pity is not the noblest of emotions, but in small doses it does no one any harm and most of us a lot of good. It is a very necessary help in times of personal bereavement, accident or sudden shock. And there are brief occasions when we all need to pretend our failures are the fault of others, or the result of hostile forces over which we have absolutely no control. Regular exposure to the sentimental melodrama of defeat will keep our neurotic anxieties comfortably relaxed, our hearts tenderized and our tear-ducts periodically flushed. They will function the more smoothly when next we need to use them in real life.

Of course, not every melodrama of defeat is sentimental. When the drowned body of her last-surviving son is brought to Maurya in Synge's *Riders to the Sea*, she does not swoon in easeful death like Steele's bereaved wife. She retains the fullest knowledge of her suffering, and accepts an irresistible defeat with dignity and courage:

They're all gone now, and there isn't anything more the sea can do to me. . . . It isn't that I haven't prayed for you, Bartley, to the Almighty God. It isn't that I haven't said prayers in the dark night till you wouldn't know what I'd be saying; but it's a great rest I'll have now, and it's time, surely. It's a great rest I'll have now, and great sleeping in the long nights after Samhain, if it's only a bit of wet flour we do have to eat, and maybe a fish that would be stinking. . . . No man at all can be living for ever, and we must be satisfied.

And this same note is heard again in melodramas of political defeat as superficially diverse as Addison's *Cato* or Robert Bolt's fine play about Sir Thomas More, *A Man for All Seasons*:

What you have hunted me for is not my actions, but the thoughts of my heart. . . . I do none harm, I say none harm, I think none harm. And if this be not enough to keep a man alive, in good faith I long not to live.

Sometimes this stoicism is replaced by fatalism. A play which shows young lovers thwarted by coincidence or chance or fate may be as sentimental as Steele's bride-and-groom tale and Hart's *Herminius and Espasia*, or as deeply persuasive as *Romeo and Juliet*, upon which Hart's play is based. Werner's *The Twenty-fourth of February* (*Der Vierundzwanzigste Februar*) derives from Lillo's *Fatal Curiosity*; but by building up a curse upon the family and focusing attention on the symbolic murder weapon on the wall, he draws from Lillo's sentimental anecdote a harrowing and fatalistic drama which established the German romantic genre of the *schicksalstragödie* ('fate-tragedy'). And when Camus took over the same plot in *Cross Purpose* (*Le Malentendu*), he used it to express the pessimistic nihilism of an existentialist philosophy which finds all life absurd and meaningless: 'this world we live in doesn't make sense' says the mother who has ignorantly killed her son. In short, the melodrama of defeat need not be sentimental, nor even second-rate. It is a form congenial to several philosophies, and has been used in many major plays. Aeschylus' *The Persians* or Euripides' *The Trojan Women* and *Iphigenia in Aulis*, the Tudor *Appius and Virginia*, *Bussy d'Ambois*, *The Duchess of Malfi*, Corneille's *Polyeucte*, Lessing's *Emilia Galotti*, Goethe's *Götz von Berlichingen* and Sartre's *Altona* will suggest themselves to many readers. These plays do not attempt to bypass the essential structure of an innocent protagonist overthrown by outside forces; they succeed because they give that framework a validity and truth which makes it answerable to our own experience. Almost daily, newspapers headline motorists in multiple collisions, pilots highjacked, diplomats abducted, pedestrians mugged or hostages and refugees gunned down by guerrillas. The melodrama of defeat chronicles all those miseries which drift towards us on the tide of hostile nature, fate or politics, war or accident or desperate men, simply because we happen to be black or Jewish or walking down the wrong street at precisely the wrong time. This is one part of our experience of reality, and the melodrama of defeat presents it truthfully as art.

At this point I must pause to slay a little dragon, for students with whom I have discussed these plays sometimes point out here that *Romeo* and *Götz* are usually thought tragedies. And Chaucer's monk would have agreed with them. 'Tragedie', he comments in the prologue to his *Tale*,

> is to seyn a certeyn storie,
> As olde bookes maken us memorie,
> Of hym that stood in greet prosperitee,
> And is yfallen out of heigh degree
> Into myserie, and endeth wrecchedly.

And he goes on to illustrate the point in a set of wretched narratives remarkably akin to Steele's. Clearly, a good man's fall from happiness to misery is common to both tragedy and melodrama, and sharper tools are needed to divide them. One root distinction, briefly sketched in Chapter 1, turns on those heroes who make a moral contribution to their fall and those who don't. In section

13 of *The Poetics*, Aristotle defines the tragic hero as a good man whose misfortune is brought upon him by some *hamartia*, which scholars have interpreted to mean a serious moral defect, intellectual blind-spot or error of judgment. All three suggest a hero who is 'with himself at war'. Orestes and Coriolanus struggle between two contradictory obligations, Macbeth and Faustus between a moral duty and a selfish desire, Hedda Gabler and Miss Julie between two selfish impulses deep in the individual personality. But Bussy and Virginia belong with Southerne's Isabella to that small band of wholly blameless souls whose downfall Aristotle thought merely shocking. The drama does not hinge upon their fatal flaws, and they are not called upon to make a moral choice between conflicting claims. Consequently, they can be toppled from their happiness only by external forces. Emilia Galotti is hounded to death by a lustful tyrant and the Duchess of Malfi by a pair of perverted evil brothers; Götz and More are persecuted by the secular authorities for their political and religious convictions, and Iphigenia sacrificed by weak men to the gods. The Trojan women and the Persians have no more control over the military maelstrom which engulfs them than does Maurya over the waves which drown her son. Such protagonists make no moral contribution to their fall. Shakespeare never hints that Romeo is wrong to fall in love with Juliet, nor she with him; the innocent lovers are destroyed rather by the feud which divides their families, by a series of unlucky accidents and by the operation of a malevolent, relentless destiny. The tragic dramatist keeps such forces in the background. Accidents like Desdemona's dropping of the handkerchief are chiefly used to accelerate rather than determine the inevitable catastrophe; and the destructive force of hostile gods or human villains is always held in check until unleashed by the hero's decisive act of frailty or folly. *Oedipus Rex* is tragic not because Oedipus is doomed by the gods but because he insists arrogantly and wilfully on uncovering the

past; Mephistophilis cannot appear to Faustus until he has turned away from God; the witches only tempt Macbeth because his heart already is attuned to them – on Banquo they have no significant effect.

Whether he creates his tragic situation for himself like Lear and Phèdre and Hedda, or is thrust into a net woven by others like Antigone and Hamlet and Othello, the tragic hero always accepts complete responsibility for what befalls him: even Macbeth and Faustus do not blame the supernatural agents who have helped in their damnation. All tragic suffering is ultimately self-inflicted, and so can lead the hero to that sudden revelation or *anagnorisis* which is the essence of the form. In the melodrama of defeat, by contrast, the hero is not master of his fate; always sinned against and never sinning, he does nothing to deserve the suffering which outside agents thrust upon him, and consequently learns from it nothing but existentialist despair, stoic resignation or Christian fortitude. Lear gains self-knowledge and a deeper understanding of experience; the Duchess of Malfi confirms her unshakable integrity. This crucial distinction between the structures of tragedy and melodrama conditions the emotional responses of an audience. The tragic hero makes heavy claims upon our sympathy. He is less than perfect and so 'like us', but he is also wrong or rash or foolish or immoral. Before we can identify with Macbeth or Oedipus we must first admit our imperfections and inadequacies. Tragedy demands of us reserves of honesty, moral courage and self-knowledge which we cannot always muster. But it costs us nothing to identify with Romeo and Juliet or with noble and courageous women like the Duchess and Iphigenia or with vigorous idealists like Götz and Thomas More. They stand for Love and Truth and Right and Honour, and are not overcome by those humiliating weaknesses we suffer in real life. We would all be as heroic and uncompromising if we could, and find it flattering to imagine for a little that we are. Then again, a tragic hero's fall releases complex feelings: pity touched by fear and awe, admiration tempered by moral reservations or even qualified by irony and laughter. *Oedipus Rex* preserves a dry mock almost to the last, and the final act of *Hamlet* finds room for foppish courtiers and gravediggers who sing of love while turning up a skull. Tragedy illuminates the contradictions of experience; melodramas of defeat are simpler and more immediately appealing. For the spectacle of totally unmerited misfortune our tears flow freely and our admiration knows no bounds. After all, such feelings cost us nothing and attest the sensibility and moral beauty of our souls. Only a handful of the greatest melodramas will allow a glimpse of sudden laughter to qualify the prevalent pathetic or heroic tone. Emotionally and morally, we are home and dry scot-free.

In short, tragedy and melodrama deal in different heroes, different conflicts, different structures and different emotional effects. Distinguishing between them is not an exercise in splitting hairs, but a means of labelling two different structures of experience. Now to stick a label on a play is dangerous when it encourages a reader not to search for the uniqueness of an individual work. The justification for little books which deal in 'tragedy' or 'melodrama' is that such labels are essential as a first step towards appreciation, for until we understand the vision of experience a dramatist is trying to convey we cannot judge of his success. Critics who stress the fatalism of *Romeo and Juliet* usually conclude the play a tragedy which fails; they would judge it very differently as a melodrama of defeat. This is not to say that Shakespeare missed the marathon and won the egg-and-spoon race. Melodrama is not inferior to tragedy; it works by different means to different ends, and comparisons are only valid when they lie within a genre. *Cato* is a failure not because it is a melodrama but because its chilly hero is a walking statue who never wins our hearts; *A Man for All Seasons* presents the conflict between an upright hero and the state with more success, but neither forms a profitable contrast with a tragedy like *Coriolanus*. Some cheeses are superior to others of their kind, but it is pointless to compare them with a lump of moon-rock. One final warning. When William Archer called Webster's *Duchess* melodrama he did not use the term as I have done to signify a unique dramatic structure. Until a coinage like 'the melodrama of defeat' gains universal currency – and I am told this may take upwards of a century – I would not recommend my reader to employ the term without a word of explanation. In popular and even academic use, *melodrama* is still a synonym for cheap and nasty thrills.

Although tragedy and melodrama spring from two opposing views of life there are many plays in which the two converge, and I should like to end this chapter with a glance at some of them. On the simplest level of collaboration are those tragedies which borrow melodrama's more sensational devices without forfeiting their own organic form. Thus Sophocles exploits the pathos of angel children in *Oedipus Rex*, Ibsen talks of scuttled ships in *Pillars of Society*, and even gentle Chekhov rescues a woman from the wheels of a stage express in *Platonov*. More interesting are tragedies with mini-melodramas of defeat written in the margin. *Macbeth* includes the melodrama of Lady Macduff almost as an independent playlet in the fourth act of the tragedy, and Ophelia in *Hamlet* sustains the same pathetic function over several scenes. Dr Rank in Ibsen's *A Doll's House* and Oswald in his *Ghosts* carry this technique further. As victims of parental syphilis they command our easy tears, but their more central placement makes this response a powerful alternative to the pursuit of tragic self-awareness undergone by Nora and Mrs Alving. In these plays Ibsen exploits the different emotional responses appropriate to tragedy and melodrama to strengthen admiration for the dedicated courage of his heroines.

A different pattern springs from melodramas where the protagonist is suddenly enriched and deepened by a glimpse of inner conflict. To revenge herself on Jason, Euripides' Medea plots to murder their two sons and the woman for whom he wishes to divorce her; suddenly she surrenders to a violent debate between maternal love and the fury of a woman scorned. Revenge predominates and the myth proceeds. Richard Crookback undergoes a similar transformation when, after three acts of joyful villainy, he gains the throne and begins to lose his grip on political events. In the tent scene before Bosworth nightmares of his murdered victims drive him into a long soliloquy of conscience and remorse which moves towards a blinkered self-discovery and gives the character a tragic stance. It does not last till morning.

Plays like Gorky's *The Lower Depths*, O'Neill's *The Iceman Cometh* and Tennessee Williams' *Small Craft Warnings* demonstrate a more deceptive melodramatic structure. All three focus on a clutch of sleazy failures in a back-room bar or squalid tenement. They live on memories of faded glory or lying hopes of a glamorous tomorrow, venture from time to time into the outside world, retreat in disarray and surrender once again to pipe-dreams, sleep and booze. To some extent these derelicts are victims of society, like Götz and Thomas More. Gorky's Pepel is a thief because his father was a thief, and Kleshch the locksmith is a willing workman ruined by industrial stagnation. The drifters of O'Neill and Williams may also make some claims against the world from which they have seceded. Yet all three dramatists leave no doubt their characters are what they are because they are too feeble to be otherwise; their failure to deal with life lies not in society but in themselves. This shift from an outer to an inner destructive agent suggests a movement into tragedy, but it is not supported by the characters' behaviour. They never suffer from the agonies of moral choice, never accept responsibility for their predicament, and never learn from their defeat. They are victims of an inner weakness as overpowering as fate or chance or nature, yet they demand – like Isabella or Monimia – that we should forgive and pity them because the world has done them wrong.

One final step brings into focus plays where tragic elements of moral choice, responsibility and self-knowledge are handled to produce effects essentially akin to melodrama. Sentimental adaptations of great tragedies provide some obvious examples. In Nahum Tate's *King Lear*, Gloster and Lear are preserved to live with Kent in blest retirement, and Cordelia rescued from the rope to find herself a Queen and Edgar's bride. 'Thy bright Example', he assures her as the curtain falls,

> Thy bright Example shall convince the World
> (Whatever Storms of Fortune are decreed)
> That Truth and Vertue shall at last succeed.

A little further wrenching, and Shakespeare's tragedy makes effective melodrama. So does Webster's *The White Devil*; when Tatified as *Injur'd Love: or, The Cruel Husband*, it opens with a sentimental melodrama of defeat emphasizing the pathetic fall of Isabella, Brachiano's innocent wronged wife. Some better versions of this 'melotragic compromise' deal with tragically divided men who prefer to think themselves pathetic victims, like Shakespeare's Richard II and Marlowe's Edward; with Elizabethan revengers distracted by dividedness who plump instead for easy blame, like Hieronimo in Kyd's *The Spanish Tragedy*, or Vindice in *The Revenger's Tragedy*, who blames the world without perceiving he is part of the corruption he would extirpate; with deluded martyrs like Musgrave in *Serjeant Musgrave's Dance*; with dupes like Willie Loman in *Death of a Salesman*, who kills himself to prove the truth of a life-time of delusion; or with magdalens and penitential prodigals whom the dramatist is eager to excuse as virtuous despite their sins. Plays in this last group oscillate so wildly between the poles of tragedy and melodrama they deserve a closer look.

At one extreme is Heywood's tragedy *A Woman Killed with Kindness*. Anne Frankford yields impetuously to her seducer, bitterly repents her sin and starves herself to death to gain salvation. Frankford forgives her on her death-bed, but neither can forget she is a strumpet. Victor's adaptation takes the opposite extreme. In *The Fatal Error* Lady Frankford repulses Cranmore 'with a proper indignation', but he gains admission to her bedroom with the help of an accomplice and rapes her while her husband is away; rather than pollute her marriage-bed, she swallows poison. Heywood's heroine regrets a moral choice and through her suffering learns wisdom; Victor's is a melodramatic innocent victimized by chance and evil men. *East Lynne* keeps a foot in either camp. Isabel is Heywood's sinning wife, but she surrenders to the reptile Levison only when he shows her 'evidence' her husband is disloyal. This palliates her moral guilt, and what remains is washed away in maudlin tears for her protracted torments. Each fresh catastrophe reminds her she is lost, abandoned, outcast, tortured, erring, mad, degraded, friendless, crippled, shattered, broken-hearted, wrecked, prematurely aged or 'alone! alone – utterly alone – for evermore!' She makes great use of 'never'. Eventually she dies in her Archibald's forgiving arms, the copybook example of a melotragic heroine. Her sisters run the usual gamut of feminine depravity. Some are ruined maidens like the beauteous Calista, who is undone by gay Lothario in Rowe's *The Fair Penitent*; others remorseful mistresses like Marguerite in *La Dame aux camélias*, a consumptive courtesan who atones for a scarlet past by renouncing her one true love and forcing him to hate her. Then there are bloodthirsty wives. 'Take this for hindering Mosbie's love and mine' cries the fiendish Alice in the Elizabethan *Arden of Feversham*; in Lillo's version she drops the dagger 'drown'd in tears' and is reconciled with Arden in a scene of rapturous forgiveness ('The flow'ry path of innocence and peace / Shines bright before, and

I shall stray no longer'). With new-born virtue, Alice tries to divert Mosby from his murderous design, is guiltless of the deed, and when arrested for complicity embraces death with adoration. *Maria Stuart* presses towards tragedy with more taste. She blames herself for Rizzio's death and Darnley's death and Bothwell's death, and so assumes responsibility for those events which lead her to the block. Yet Schiller fastens in the memory another portrait, of a guiltless queen stripped of her train, her liberty and title, illegally imprisoned, betrayed by headstrong or faint-hearted friends, and executed for political necessity upon the strength of perjured evidence in a trumped-up charge. Such ambivalence is the hallmark of the melotragic compromise.

Most penitential prodigals are more overtly sentimental. Consider, for example, gamblers like Bellmour in Hill's *The Fatal Extravagance* or Beverley in Edward Moore's *The Gamester*, who dices his estate away and then takes poison; or young Barnwell, the honest clerk of Lillo's *The London Merchant*, who falls in with a courtesan, embezzles money, kills his uncle and gives himself up to the law. Potentially, all three are tragic heroes like Macbeth – men who knowingly embrace a wrongful course, are racked with guilt, repent too late and die made wise by suffering. Yet all three are seen through sentimental spectacles by dramatists who condemn the hero's crime and then feel free to build up pity for his miseries. All tragic guilt is bleached away. With touching altruism, Bellmour commits murder only to keep his friend from prison, and tries to poison his wife and children only to preserve them all from beggary. Human villains also do their bit. Beverley's innate 'spark of folly' is assiduously kindled by revengeful Stukely ('I cheat him, and he calls me Friend'), and Barnwell's downfall wholly blamed on Millwood, an evil siren who in turn blames her vicious life upon society. And, of course, all three protagonists are plagued with rotten luck. Bellmour and Beverley learn of a rich inheritance just too late to prevent their suicide, and Barnwell has just decided not to kill his uncle when he drops the pistol, alarms the good old man, and is forced to stab him to forestall discovery. When moral guilt thus becomes an accident of virtue, the hero who insists on shouldering it himself finds our pity mounting evenly with his remorse. Because he blames himself, we are unable to blame him. Beverley, poor man, wanders through the play 'loaded with every Curse, that drives the Soul to Desperation', and Barnwell sheds so many tears 'o'er each Offence, as might, if possible, sanctify Theft, and make a Merit of a Crime'. Pardon is their dearest wish. They intercalate every crime with resolutions of reform, and beat their breasts in anguish every time they are betrayed into some fresh murder, robbery or game of dice. Their deaths are lovely. Visited in prison by loyal friends, weeping sweet-hearts and forgiving wives, they indulge in ecstasies of grief which spread like wild fire round the cast. 'Look down with Mercy on his Sorrows!' begs Mrs Beverley,

> . . . Take from his Memory the Sense of what is past, and cure him of Despair! On Me! on Me! if Misery must be the Lot of either, multiply Misfortunes!

Barnwell does even better. The fairest maid that London boasts 'kindly condescends' to weep for his unhappy fate, and honest Trueman lies down beside him on the cold, cold stones, to mingle tears and sighs and mutual groans which 'eccho to each other thro' the dreary Vault'. This is the attitude the dramatist is asking us to share, and we are lucky to escape with easy tears. A late addition to the play takes Barnwell to the scaffold, where he wrestles like a priest with the despair of Millwood's soul. To gain such scenes, the hero's tragic nature has been utterly destroyed, and the melotragic compromise turned back into the sentimental melodrama of defeat with which this chapter started.

4
Protest

Protest theatre has many aims: to stimulate political awareness, question established values, expose injustice, champion reform, fuel arguments on ways and means and sometimes to incite direct support for bloody revolution. The result may be a satire, homily, cartoon, revue or straight-play-with-a-message, but underneath the fashionable trimmings the essential form is melodrama. Take, for example, the crusading hero up in arms against some manifest corruption. A whiff of indecision would destroy his moral stature and might induce his followers to think again; crushing every private doubt, he declares himself wholeheartedly devoted to a cause he says is just, and fights for Right against those necessarily external forces symbolizing Wrong. And since no compromise is possible between such mighty opposites, the drama always ends in triumph or defeat. Either serves to rally new supporters to The Cause, and both provide a satisfying, simplified *catharsis*. Victory can be enjoyed only by blocking off our sympathy for those who are defeated, and defeat arouses righteous anger at the world's injustices unmitigated by the thought that we may also be to blame. This melodramatic structure of experience is shared by protest plays as different as *Prometheus Bound* and Ibsen's *An Enemy of the People*. Prometheus is the rebel Titan who brought Man fire and for this act was shackled to a rock by Zeus' command. Aeschylus presents him as the fearless champion of freedom, unjustly victimized by a dictator and sustained across millennia of anguish by the secret knowledge of his enemy's eventual destruction. Ibsen confines the conflict to a small Norwegian township. When Dr Stockmann announces that the town spa is polluted, a cabal of vested interests has him silenced, sacked, evicted and declared a public enemy. Again, it is an over-simple conflict: the villains are totally devoted to expedient self-interest, and Stockmann is so dazzled by the blinding light of Truth he never stops to estimate the moral stature of the men with whom he deals. Like Prometheus he has his limitations, but the dramatist deploys them only to dispel that priggishness which readily attaches to the man who knows that he is right. They are not allowed to qualify our admiration for his courage or our righteous indignation at his outrageous fall.

Patterns of social protest fit so snugly into melodrama that few nineteenth-century examples can resist a random fling at some *bête noire*, from pressgangs or the poor laws down to prostitution or the gross malpractices of private lunatic asylums. And no one bothers if these diatribes intrude upon exciting situations when attention should be focused somewhere else. In *Under the Gaslight*, Byke ties Snorkey to the railway line and Laura is locked up in a hut beside the track; she breaks out with a handy axe, and drags him – only just in time – from the thundering express. 'Victory!' he chortles, 'Saved! Hooray! And these are the women who ain't to have a vote!' Sometimes whole plays are structured to expose a significant injustice. *Uncle Tom's Cabin* campaigns for abolition, with an unscrupulous slave-hunter precipitated from a cliff-top ('Friend, thee is not wanted here!') and a gentle Bible-punching nigger hero flogged to death by the command of villainous Legree. Over his body the French version has a senator declare that there are still some amendments to be introduced into the law. The second act of Reade's *It's Never Too Late to Mend* is given over to the borough gaol. The governor is a sadistic psychopath whose penal code grinds prisoners to bone-dust, his chaplain is 'the friend of suffering humanity' and the convicts are their battleground. When Robinson is too weak to finish working on the treadmill, the governor removes his

F

bed and light and puts him onto bread and water – 'and short allowance of that'. Young Josephs is a saintly innocent who stole a handful of potatoes to feed his starving mother. In prison he is beaten, famished, crushed in a punishment jacket and drenched in buckets of cold water; when he dies the chaplain begs Robinson never to despair. Still more ferocious is *The Factory Lad*, which deals with a group of honest weavers made redundant by the new steam-looms. Poaching, emigration and the workhouse are canvassed and dismissed as answers to their penury. In desperate revenge they fire the factory, smash the looms, and are brought to trial by Justice Bias. The sneering factory owner is shot dead by a poacher, and the wreckers left to trial and execution as the curtain falls. There is no happy ending here, no songs, no jokes, no light relief and precious little pathos; this savage protest drama is a grim tract for grim times. Despite the great variety of tone, all three plays adopt a common strategy: to pinpoint a contemporary evil they set up a blameless hero as the victim of the system, and then subject him to such inhuman persecution that the audience explodes with indignation and demands the immediate repeal of laws which perpetrate such cruelties.

In this, of course, they are wholly unsuccessful. Protest melodrama speaks exclusively to the converted; *The Factory Lad* was played for six nights only to an audience of workers on the seamy side of London, and Uncle Tom was never seen in public south of the Mason–Dixon line. Such plays may focus discontent, fire public feeling and congratulate their audience on siding with the angels, but they are too vehemently partisan, too shrill and facile in denunciation, to persuade the uncommitted man of even moderate intelligence that their black and white world is the grey one that he knows. Effective protest takes account of these complexities. Compare Reade's prison drama with a problem play like *Justice*. Galsworthy is not trapped into a cheap antithesis; his prison officers are decent chaps with the best intentions, and his convict is a moral weakling sent down for petty forgery. The wordless scene of Falder's solitary confinement harrows not because he is a victim of grotesque injustice but because we feel no penal system ought to treat a man this way. Young Winston Churchill was so shaken by it that he steered through Parliament some long overdue reforms. Galsworthy's ability to show a social evil 'in the round', without surrendering to the simplistic patterns of the protest melodrama, animates all problem plays which deserve the title, from *Strife*, a study of industrial unrest in which the viewpoints of both capital and labour are sympathetically presented, down to Shaw's attack on prostitution in *Mrs Warren's Profession* and John Arden's satire on the Welfare State re-housing scheme in *Live like Pigs*.

The problem play appeals to thinking men; the protest melodrama to men who wish to think that they are thinking while their prejudices are pampered. It has always been the more popular form. During the depression years agitprop companies, dedicated to agitational propaganda on the pattern of the Russian workers' troupes, toured the cities of America with crude melodramas which exposed the social evils of a decadent capitalism. At the premiere of Odets' *Waiting for Lefty* in 1935, actors playing militants in a taxi-drivers' union were joined on stage by members of the audience in one great cry of 'Strike!' London's Rebel Players stole the script the same October, and then amalgamated with Red Radio to form the Unity Theatre; their later work included *The Fall of the House of Slusher*, about an extortionate capitalist overthrown by his employees. More recently, Joan Littlewood's left-wing Theatre Workshop presented *The Projector*, an inflammatory attack upon unscrupulous property development based on the Ronan Point disaster and disguised, for legal reasons, as a ballad opera written in 1733 by one William Rufus Chetwood. Two years ago in Paris Ariane Mnouchkine's Théâtre du Soleil celebrated the people's revolution of *1789*;

as the Bastille fell the entire auditorium was transformed into a fairground festival ablaze with joy and light and laughter and triumphal music. America is currently supporting three outstanding theatres of protest. The San Francisco Mime Troupe update scenarios from the *commedia dell'arte* to point a revolutionary moral. Richard Schechner's Guerrilla Theater stage happenings which antagonize an audience into a new radical awareness. The parables of El Teatro Campesino strengthen solidarity among the Union of Farm Workers from Southern California; they have already won better wages from their employers.

In totalitarian societies, which put to silence voices raised against established values, the patterns of the protest melodrama are inverted to produce those propaganda plays which laud the *status quo* as eagerly as Western protest groups denounce it. Witness, for example, Lenin's hagiolatry in *Kremlin Chimes*. All around is famine and the aftermath of war, but the people's hero (haloed by a cunning sunbeam) hobnobs with the peasantry and talks over with the head of his political police a mighty plan to spread electric power through the land. When the Great Proletarian Cultural Revolution got under way in 1965, the ancient stories of the Chinese opera were replaced by model pieces to support the revolution and foster solidarity among the workers who make up this 'new society'. *Taking Tiger Mountain by Strategy* shows a detachment of the People's Army beating a bandit chief called Vulture during the Third Revolutionary War. In *Shachiapang* Fourth Army soldiers are helped by kindly villagers to conquer puppet troops. *The Red Lantern* has a party member giving up his life to send a secret message to guerrillas while hemmed in by the invading Japanese. Dressed in red, apparently to emphasize his courage, the hero takes up a dominant position on the symbolic stage; the light plays brightly on his features, and he gestures with an amplitude beyond the reach of naturalism. The general effect must be remarkably akin to that produced by noble George in the Victorian melodrama of triumph – which is, of course, what most of these plays are.

In the West the protest theatre appeals today to militant minorities in basements underneath the Paris boulevards, in Soho pubs and attics, in the bars of Greenwich Village or the back-streets of San Francisco. The national theatres of East Berlin and Moscow tell a different story. China in 1965 had 600 million workers and about 3,000 theatre companies, all but 200 of them devoted to operas and ballads. It is, in fact, difficult to resist the view that melodrama reaches now a wider audience than any in its history. And this is as it should be, for there is no other form of theatre which speaks so simply and directly to the people as a whole.

Bibliography and Acknowledgements

Two indispensable works of reference are *The London Stage 1660–1800*, ed. W. VAN LENNEP, E. L. AVERY, A. H. SCOUTEN, G. WINCHESTER STONE JR. and C. B. HOGAN (Carbondale, Illinois, 1960–68), and ALLARDYCE NICOLL's *A History of English Drama 1660–1900* (Cambridge, 1923–46, later revised); a separate volume of the latter surveys *English Drama: 1900–1930* (Cambridge, 1973).

ERIC BENTLEY devotes a chapter to melodrama in *The Life of the Drama* (London, 1965), and JAMES L. ROSENBERG defends the form in *The Context and Craft of Drama*, ed. ROBERT W. CORRIGAN and JAMES L. ROSENBERG (San Francisco, 1964). Two other general studies are WYLIE SYPHER's 'Aesthetic of revolution: the Marxist melodrama' in *The Kenyon Review*, X (Summer, 1948), 431–44, and ROBERT BECHTOLD HEILMAN's 'Tragedy and melodrama: speculations on generic form' in *The Texas Quarterly*, III (Summer, 1960), 36–50. All four pieces are reprinted in *Tragedy: Vision and Form*, ed. ROBERT W. CORRIGAN (San Francisco, 1965), and PROFESSOR HEILMAN's article forms the basis of his stimulating book *Tragedy and Melodrama: Versions of Experience* (Seattle and London, 1968). Also valuable is ROBERT W. CORRIGAN's introduction to *The Laurel British Drama: the Nineteenth Century* (New York, 1967). These works have been at my elbow during the writing of this monograph. I hope I have acknowledged in the text all direct quotation from them but, as Bentley himself observes, 'one may quote the most cherished author least because one has absorbed his thought so well one considers it one's own'. My apologies to any I have repaid so ungratefully.

Most of the eighteenth-century plays discussed in Chapter 3 are treated in ERNEST BERNBAUM's pioneering study *The Drama of Sensibility* (New York, 1915), and ARTHUR SHERBO's *English Sentimental Drama* (Michigan, 1957). The best studies of nineteenth-century melodrama are PAUL GINISTY's *Le Mélodrame* (Paris, 1910), MICHAEL BOOTH's *English Melodrama* (London, 1965) and DAVID GRIMSTED's *Melodrama Unveiled: American Theater and Culture 1800–1850* (Chicago and London, 1968). FRANK RAHILL's *The World of Melodrama* (Pennsylvania and London, 1967) deals thoroughly with French, English and American melodrama and contains a valuable bibliography. My information on film melodrama comes from DANIEL BLUM's *A Pictorial History of the Silent Screen* (London, 1962) and *A Pictorial History of the Talkies* revised by JOHN KOBAL (London, 1968). For the protest plays discussed in Chapter 4 I am indebted to several articles in *Theatre Quarterly*, I (Winter, 1971), and to JOHN LAHR's *Acting out America* (London, 1972).

One reason so little has been written upon melodrama is that the plays themselves are difficult to come by. Translations of Aeschylus, Sophocles and Euripides are readily available, and Shakespeare may be read in PETER ALEXANDER's one-volume edition (Glasgow and London, 1951). Separate plays are fully annotated in the New Arden series, while the Revels Plays provide this service for. many Elizabethan and Jacobean titles. Two compendious anthologies are *English Drama 1580–1642*, ed. C. F. TUCKER BROOKE and NATHANIEL BURTON PARADISE (Boston, 1933) and *Elizabethan and Stuart Plays*, ed. CHARLES READ BASKERVILL, VIRGIL B. HELTZEL and ARTHUR H. NETHERCOT (New York and London, 1934). *Cato, The Fair Penitent, The Beggar's Opera, The School for Scandal, The Stranger, The London Merchant* and *Douglas* are in *Plays of the*

Restoration and Eighteenth Century, ed. DOUGALD MACMILLAN and HOWARD MUMFORD JONES (New York and London, 1931), and MICHAEL BOOTH's *Eighteenth Century Tragedy* (London, 1965) reprints the last two with *Irene* and *The Gamester*. Some individual titles are available in the Regents Restoration Drama Series. Pixerécourt's *Cœlina* is in *Nineteenth Century French Plays*, ed. JOSEPH L. BORGERHOFF (New York and London, 1931), and *Uncle Tom's Cabin* in *Representative Plays by American Dramatists*, ed. MONTROSE J. MOSES (New York, 1918–25). Fechter's *Monte Cristo* may be read in *Great Melodramas*, ed. ROBERT SAFFRON (New York, 1966), together with *Gaslight* under its American title, *Angel Street*. GEORGE ROWELL's *Nineteenth Century Plays* (London, 1953, revised 1972) includes *Black-ey'd Susan*, *The Colleen Bawn*, HAZLEWOOD's *Lady Audley's Secret*, *The Ticket-of-Leave Man* and *The Bells*. In *Hiss the Villain* MICHAEL BOOTH prints *The Miller and his Men*, *My Poll and My Partner Joe*, *Ten Nights in a Bar-Room*, *Lost in London*, *Under the Gaslight* and *The Bells* (London, 1964); his two-volume collection of *English Plays of the Nineteenth Century* (Oxford, 1969) includes *The Miller and his Men*, *Black-ey'd Susan*, *The Factory Lad*, *The Corsican Brothers*, *The Ticket-of-Leave Man* and *The Shaughraun*. JAMES L. SMITH's *The Drunkard and Other Melodramas* (London, 1973) contains MILNER's version of *Mazeppa*, *The Factory Lad*, *Nick of the Woods*, *The Drunkard*, *London by Night*, *The Corsican Brothers* and *The Lady of the Camellias*. The twenty volumes of *America's Lost Plays*, ed. BARRETT H. CLARK (Princeton, 1940–49) also contain many melodramas. For others, the reader must fall back upon the collected works of Pixerécourt (Paris, 1841–43), Dumas *père* (Paris, 1863–74), Bulwer-Lytton (London, 1841), Henry Arthur Jones (Boston, 1925) and Tom Taylor (London, 1854, 1877), and the hideously printed acting texts of the period, now rarely found outside the great national libraries.

BIBLIOGRAPHY AND ACKNOWLEDGEMENTS 81

The principal collections are Cumberland's British Theatre (London, 1826–61), Cumberland's Minor Theatre (London, 1828–43), Dicks' Standard Plays (London, 1875 ff.), Duncombe's British Theatre (London, 1828–52), Lacy's Acting Edition (London, 1849–55) continued as French's Acting Edition (London and New York, still current), Oxberry's Edition (London, 1818–23), Pattie's Play (London, 1838–39), Michel-Lévy Frères' Théâtre Contemporain Illustré (Paris, 1840–75) and Webster's Acting National Drama (London, 1837–59). Thousands of unprinted melodramas are preserved in the Bibliothèque de l'Arsenal at Paris, the Library of Congress, the Huntington Library at San Marino, California, and the British Museum; those who cannot reach these collections must depend upon the reviews in contemporary newspapers and magazines. *The Stage Directory* began as a monthly in February 1880 and has continued weekly as *The Stage* from March 1881. CLEMENT SCOTT's *The Theatre* was published monthly between 1877 and 1897; BERNARD SHAW's *Dramatic Opinions and Essays* (New York, 1916) reprints articles first published in *The Saturday Review* between January 1895 and May 1898.

G

Index of Proper Names

Index of Titles

This index lists all the plays mentioned in the text. Each title is followed by the author's name and, where appropriate, by the title of the play from which it was adapted (ad). Then comes the year of first performance, followed for plays written after 1660 by an indication of where it can be found. Separate editions are shown by a date (or an asterisk if this is the same as the year of first performance); acting editions and anthologies by an initial (B = Booth's *Eighteenth Century Tragedy*; B2 = *Hiss the Villain*; B3 = Booth's *English Plays*; C = Cumberland; CM = Cumberland Minor; D = Dicks; Dun = Duncombe; F = French; L = Lacy; MJ = MacMillan and Jones; O = Oxberry; P = Pattie; R = Rowell; S = Smith; TCI = *Théâtre Contemporain Illustré*; W = Webster; details of these editions are given in the bibliography). Unpublished plays in the British Museum are marked BM; plays mentioned on the evidence of contemporary playbills or reviews are initialled PB or RE. For modern European classics I give details of the standard English translation (ET). Film titles are followed by the names of the studio and director (d), when these are known, and by the year of release. For television series, the distributing channel is given.